M000302753

Anticipatory Grief

The Journey of a Thousand Losses and Endless Grace

by Tracy K. Pratt

Anticipatory Grief

Copyright © 2019 Tracy K. Pratt
All rights reserved.
ISBN: 978-1-945976-42-1

Scriptures from the THE HOLY BIBLE, NEW INTERNATIONAL
VERSION ®. Copyright© 1973, 1978, 1984, 2011 by Biblica, Inc.™. Used by
permission of Zondervan.

Published by EA Books Publishing a division of
Living Parables of Central Florida, Inc. a 501c3
EABooksPublishing.com

Dedication

To the most important women in my life:

Evelyn H Kent, my mother,
Reva Pratt, my mother-in-law,
Hannah Pratt, my daughter,

each taught me much about anticipatory grief
on their courageous journeys before they died.

Teresa Pratt, my daughter-in-law,
you are my friend and companion
in faith, motherhood and marriage.
I am grateful.

Contents

Acknowledgements

Six years. That is the gestation period of this book. The time has been well spent in the company of mentors, fellow-creatives and encouragers named below. Though my name is on the cover, each has left their mark in the book.

Coleman, my relentless and loudest cheerleader, thank you for listening. You have been my most valuable advisor. Thank you for your patient attention when I interrupt your morning ritual with a stream of thought that has been stirring well before dawn—which is almost every day. Thank you for believing in the vision when I doubted, and thank you for praying over me. Your undeterred confidence in God's call has sustained me.

JP, your own adventures in business and family life inspire me to push through and keep relevant. I treasure our creative camaraderie. Thank you for celebrating my small and big successes. You, Teresa, and the children refresh my spirit.

Larry and Rachael, thank you for friendship that is founded on the hope of the unseen. I am grateful for its timing. Thank you for conversations and presence in the arduous journey.

Debbie Burton, Loretta Schoen, Yvette Bishop, and Vickie Hudnall, how good to have you as my fellow pilgrims in life as well as writing. Debbie, what a privilege to share in each other's highs and lows of the writing and publishing journey. Loretta, who would have imgagined, one weekend 600 hundred miles away, God would bring us together at a marketing conference? Now, here we are living just a few miles apart, encouraging one another in the steps we take. Yvette, thank you for your abiding faith since the beginning. The meme you created for me from Isaiah 41:10 has been a constant reminder of God's faithfulness to accomplish what He has planned, and, that you pray for me. Vickie, my long time friend, thank you for praying and for being present when your life has been difficult. Thank you for your active interest and feedback.

My fellow-creatives at Word Weavers Intl., Orlando and Word Weavers Online Group, Page 9, thank you for your honest and encouraging critiques month after month. Thank you for persevering in your own work. You gave, and continue to give strength through community. I treasure the memory of the day I brought the first 2000 words for critiquing. Chanda, Dondi, and Linda, your encouraging words fertilized the idea of autumn as the metaphor for anticipatory grief. Your personal reactions nurtured the passion to educate and encourage other women in the journey.

Cheri Cowell, thank you for your sense of expectancy from conception through the production of the book. And, thank you for the vision of EA Publishing. I am one of the many authors you envisioned when your dream was just a seed.

EA Publishing production team: Kristen Veldhuis, Project Coordinator; Dawn Staymates, Formatting Specialist; Bob Ousnamer, Conversion Specialist – Cover Designer – Marketing Coach; Dale Lipscomb, Editor, thank you for listening to the concept. With objective and experienced eyes, you took my words, and shaped this message of grace others now hold in their hands. Thank you for your commitment.

Michele Penny, Melanie Bowden, Russell Kent, Teresa Pratt, and Terry Scancella thank you for being my Beta readers, my test audience. Your insight, edits, and remarks provided a fresh and much-needed perspective. Thank you for your willingness and for the time you devoted to the project.

Thank you to Grace Journey Community Church for your prayers, interest, and excitement. You have been life-companions and prayer warriors long before and during the gestation of this book.

Carey, Imgard, Sally, and Kathryn, and Vickie thank you for courageously sharing with the audience. Thank you for being a voice for others. Thank you to the nameless individuals whose role in my anticipatory grief story are in the book. Each of you did what came naturally to you. Little did you know, as God's workmanship, you were grace-givers, walking into a situation for which He equipped you, and we were the recipients.

Brown Dances Down

A Poem Dedicated to Grief

Tracy K. Pratt

Green pales Yellow
Then blushes Brown
Broken from stem
Brown dances down

Naked to rain
Beaten by sun
Tossed in the wind
Brown is undone

Supple to brittle
Whispers to sighs
Breath heaves little
Aching Brown lies

Torn over time
Brown curls and dies
Buried in white
The wind alone cries

White disappears
Sun warms Brown's tomb
Rain and wind kiss
Make Brown Green's tomb

Green births Yellow
Purple and Red
They dance in the wind
Where Brown lay dead [1]

Anticipatory Grief

The Journey of a Thousand Losses and Endless Grace

by Tracy K. Pratt

The Why of Anticipatory Grief

Green pales Yellow
Then blushes Brown
Broken from stem
Brown dances down[2]

CHAPTER 1

Once Upon a Time

They lived happily ever after
– a classic fairy tale ending –

"Have you ever experienced moments of fullness," I asked a few of my friends, "that sense of 'Ah, this is the way things should be'?"

One answered, "Tiny, fleeting moments that explode out of the exhausting chaos of most days."

"Decluttering," a second friend said. "A sense of freedom from being tied down to too many things."

A third added, "Finding lost things."

The earth has an "ahhh" moment in summer, when it leans closest to the sun and the air is rich with humidity. It laughs. The sun beams, "This is the way things should be." Water courses through Earth's veins and the sun's golden light chases it. Where the two kiss, everything is green.

January 23, 1982

My heart laughed. After eleven laborious hours, she arrived, a wrinkled, scrawny, eighteen-and-a-half inch long doll. The doctor laid her on my stomach. Skin-to-skin, we melded.

"Is she real?" I asked.

He chuckled. "Why, yes. Every inch of her."

A thin veneer of white clung to her mottled skin and a clump of matted hair topped her skull. Ten miniature porcelain fingers clawed the air as five pounds, three ounces of nakedness squirmed on my chest. I stretched my hand to touch my newborn daughter. Her head filled my palm. Her breath warmed my fingers. Her wail pierced my heart. The inexplicable rightness of motherhood wove an indestructible web between us.

In that brief touch, I promised my daughter everything I had imagined as a five-year-old girl.

On Saturdays, I used to play house in my attic room while the rest of the family slept late. Some mornings I painted my dolls' faces with crayons and forced their coiffed hair into new 'dos. Then, I dressed them in frills and shoes. After the primp, I propped the three against pillows set in a semicircle on the throw rug.

"Suzie, you sit here. Annie, sit there. Oh, no! No-no. Baby! Don't crawl away. Come back. Ewww, do you need a diaper change?"

I picked up Baby, patted her back, then set her down again with Suzie and Annie.

"Oh, don't cry. Have some tea. Is that better?"

I poured water from the teapot into thimble-sized cups glued to saucers. The doll's legs protruded in front of them like rubber logs. I opened a picture book, telling the story my way. My captive audience stared ahead as I gave each a good look at the double-paged illustrations. Their applause perpetually suspended in mid-air.

My dream never faded. The longing sown in my heart grew like the perpetual green of an endless summer. In adolescence, mothers entrusted me with their babies and children for a night or a weekend. I worked at camps, and at children's clubs during summers in college.

That dreary January afternoon in 1982, happiness drenched me like grass sopping with dew on an August day. A nurse whisked my newborn daughter away to be cleaned. Another wheeled me into recovery. Back in my hospital room, I lived for our reunion.

Propped against three pillows, my eyes flitted to the doorway at each sound of a cart. My arms lay open on my lap, waiting. Finally, squeaky wheels stopped in the doorway, and a nurse wheeled a bassinet into the room. I sat straighter, leaned forward. She transferred my daughter to my outstretched arms. I settled back, cradling her securely to my breast.

"Ah, here you are."

My lips brushed a kiss on her forehead and trickled six words into her ear.

"I love you, Hannah Michelle Pratt."

Her warmth blazed a deep satisfaction through me.

Yes! This is how things should be!

My eyes closed, my head bent in thanksgiving.

Where did my "Ahhh" moment come from? Where does anyone's? Satisfaction erupts when our hearts brim with delight, when everything seems right in our personal worlds.

Everything complete. Nothing broken.

No death. No grief.

Once upon a time everything was as it should be — happily ever after—for the first woman in the Garden of Eden. Our moments of happiness echo what once was a normal day for her.

Sunlight sneaked over the horizon and through a hedge of branches, then kissed Eve's eyelids. Sleep drifted away. She stretched. Her back bumped into Adam's. Smiling, she turned, fitted her body into his curled one, and wrapped her right arm around his chest. He stirred and pressed closer, his right hand covering hers. Their skin lightly kissed. Happiness replaced sleepiness and she moved closer.

Another day with him. *What shall we do? Where shall we go? What will we find?* Every day Adam introduced her to a new creature, or they discovered more life in the garden. She grinned at the memory of yesterday's discoveries. They had found a nest of baby birds.

She opened her eyes. Rising from their bed of leaves, she emerged from their haven of trees. A chorus of birdsongs stirred the air. Sunlight painted the garden gold. Flower stems bowed eagerly to the queen of the garden as she brushed passed them. The pear tree dripped with fruit. One hung as if waiting for just the moment she would pass. She picked it absentmindedly and sank her teeth into the savory flesh.

Her thoughts flew with anticipation to another evening walk with God at the end of day. As much as she adored Adam, she worshipped God.

"He loves me."

She shook her head with wonder and imagined her first sight of Him kneeling over her. Waiting. Laughing. She extended her arms, and lifted her face skyward.

"My creator! I will see him at sunset."

She wandered to the edge of the field at the center of the garden and stopped. The waist-high grass encircled the most unique trees of all creation. Neither the shade of a live oak, the haven of the kapok, nor the fragrance and bloom of wisteria could compare to the beauty of these two trees. They were king and queen of all the trees.

Adam first brought her here after God introduced them. She paused and closed her eyes picturing her husband's first look. His eyes blazed with a mixture of surprise and delight. Recognition etched his face.

She laughed aloud recalling his first words "Wow! This is what came from me! Like me, oh, but certainly not me!"

His hands cupped, then tilted her face toward him. "I will call you, 'Woman,'" he said, wrapping his arms around her and pulling her close.

God chuckled. "Go, Adam. Take her. Give her what I have given both of you. Enjoy! The earth belongs to you and your kind."

They laughed. Adam and Eve hugged Him.

Adam grabbed her hand then pulled her through the garden to this field with the two trees. Their color and fragrance had taken her breath away. Fruit flooded their branches. A plethora of birds flitted in and out of the foliage. Eve walked away from Adam toward the tree on the left, but he caught her right hand with both of his and pulled her back.

"No. We must not eat of that tree. God said we could eat of any tree in the garden except that one." He spun away from her with hands in the air, then walked slowly back. "If we eat the fruit we will surely die. He called it the 'Tree of Knowledge of Good and Evil.' Best to admire it from a distance. Let's enjoy everything else." He made a sweeping gesture of the garden and sky that ended with her hands in his, and his eyes looking into hers.

"What is die, Adam?"

"I don't know. All I know is our Beloved said not to eat from it. The look on His face and the sound of his voice tells me 'die' is nothing like Him or being with Him. And nothing like this."

"What is good?"

"Oh," his voice rang with certainty. "God is good. Everything He gives and speaks is good. Even His words of warning."

She eyed the one tree, then the other.

"It looks just as beautiful and delicious as that one."

"I know." Adam pulled her to the other tree. He picked a piece of fruit from a low branch, bit off a chunk, and offered her the rest. The nectar exploded in her mouth as she took a nibble.

"This is soooooo good."

"It is, isn't it? Best fruit ever. This is the Tree of Life. We can eat from it all the time. Anytime. And Eve?"

"Mm?" The juice from the fruit dripped from Eve's fingers. She had been busy collecting every drop with her tongue, when he grabbed her hands and pivoted her around and around into the field. They tumbled into the grass.

Eve caught her breath remembering the joy of what happened next. *Oh, yes! What the Beloved gave was good.*

Afterward, her head pillowed on his chest, she asked, "Adam?"

"Hmm?" His eyes were closed.

"What is evil?"

"I don't know, but I would think it would be different than God. Way different than this." He kissed her.

The rising sun's radiance now blinded her eyes, jostling her thoughts to the present. She ambled into the grass. The wet silken blades slid through her open hands and brushed her legs. The sun in the morning mist etched the trees' silhouettes in gold. Of all the trees in the garden, she preferred eating the fruit from the Tree of Life. And she liked it best when she and Adam shared a piece of fruit together. The nectar seemed sweeter.

The thought made her stop and turn to retrace her steps, but a rustle from the mist arrested her attention. The crown of the Tree of Knowledge of Good and Evil shook, and a shower of dew cascaded through the mist, breaking it apart. Intrigued, she walked closer. Stopped. A voice disturbed her curiosity.

"Eve ... Eve ..."

Was that Adam?

She turned, again, searching the edge of the clearing. No, Adam was not there.

"Eve ... Eve ..."

Could it be God?

She dismissed the thought with a smile. She knew his voice. And, if God had come early, all the birds stirring nearby would swarm filling the field with song. There was only one solitary sound. Her name.

"Eve ... Eve ... Eve ..."

Where was the voice coming from? From the trees, perhaps?

She tiptoed into the broken mist. [3]

Once upon a time goodness reigned on the earth. The hearts of the earth's king and queen beat in rhythm with God's. Two minds filled with unending vision and unerring reason like His. In unison, two souls exhaled pure delight and satisfaction in Him.

Adam and Eve knew nothing of "should be" or "could be" with which we are so intimately acquainted. Unfading green graced their world. Harmony and flawless love bloomed between God, humans, and the earth. Every day brimmed with innocence. The idyllic was not wishful thinking, but normal life. Forever.

Eden was not a fairy tale, but the beginning of the human story—your story and mine.

Things were as they should be. There was no death and no grief - not even the concept.

That is hard for us to imagine. The innocence of a newborn is the closest we come to the innocence of Eden. All too soon the awareness of pain invades a child's world as innocuous as random bad dream to the tragedy of abuse.

So what went wrong?

When Adam and Eve ate fruit from the forbidden tree, death entered the human soul and invaded everything God created.

Oneness with God vaporized. The experience of happily ever after died, but the ache for it remained.

Flashes of *"Ahh, this is the way things should be"* come when we taste goodness as small as a nibble of dark chocolate or as significant as the birth of a child. Happiness runs through our veins and contentment washes over us. Things as they should be do happen. Every goodness, no matter how tiny, or short, blows into our souls and stirs eternity.

Our hearts dance.

Mine did.

Not quite twenty-four hours old, my baby slept, cocooned in a thin flannel blanket and a stocking cap secure in her daddy's arms. Coleman, my husband, half sat on the hospital bed. His left arm a nest for Hannah's head. The white noise of referee whistles, and the roar of the Super Bowl XVI crowd droned from the television. During commercials his gaze reverted to his bundle and he bent to kiss her forehead.

"Hello, Hannah," he would whisper. "I'm your daddy."

I leaned against the embankment of pillows. The back of my head sank into them and my blanketed legs stretched before me. I dozed, tired from the labor the day before and a euphoric night after, yet reluctant to sleep. What if I missed a finger curl? A smile?

Snippets of our nine-month wait ran through my mind. I loved reviewing one in particular. Many mornings in the third trimester, before Coleman and I got out of bed, movement rippled under my stretched abdomen. The child seemed to ask, "I don't hear voices. Are you still there?"

Coleman rested his hand over the movement. I lay holding my breath.

"Ahhh, Yes!" my heart sang.

Gene by gene, tissue by tissue, God knitted this little person in the womb. The thought that this baby was designed by Him with love stirred my happiness. We were confident the child, however formed, would bring applause from God.

We whispered and giggled those mornings with the eagerness of young children waiting to open presents Christmas morning.

"Just wait," God said. "I'm making someone, just for you."

Now, sleeping in Daddy's arms, here she was. His gift to us. And the gift was good ... but not what we expected.

CHAPTER 2

Things Are Not As They Should Be

*"If I find in myself a desire which nothing
in this world can satisfy, the most logical explanation is that I was
made for another world [4]*
– C. S. Lewis –

Have you eyed the shape of a gift with hope, only to open it and be disappointed?. Perhaps the giver meant to give the item to someone else? Or, the much-anticipated present is broken. Sometimes, we receive something personal that is not to our taste, or is the wrong size.

The heart responds, "Oh, this is not good."

Mine trembled as my mother-in-law—a nurse—said, "Something is wrong with this baby. I've changed Hannah's diaper too many times today."

Hannah was three weeks old.

"No," I countered. "Absolutely not. Nothing is wrong with her. It must be from breast feeding. They say breast-fed babies poop a lot."

Decisive words, but fear squeezed my heart. I had noticed something odd about Hannah's eyes. Yesterday they shone sky blue. Today they hid under puffy jaundiced eyelids. Was that normal for a newborn? Were they like that after a nap? Before? I couldn't remember.

Please God, don't let it be. Please, let it be paranoia. No, I will not tell Mom what I've noticed.

My mother-in-law's observation heightened my attention to detail the next few days. How often did she eat? How much? How often did I change her diaper? Was Mom right? Perhaps these peculiarities were unique to Hannah and not signs of something wrong.

Her one month checkup is a week from Monday. I will talk to her pediatrician then.

Hope loosened the grip in my chest.

During my pregnancy, people often asked Coleman and me, "What do you want? A boy or a girl?"

"It doesn't matter," we answered.

"Oh, I get it," they responded. "Just as long as it's healthy."

Is it wrong to want a healthy baby or marriage, or a successful career? Of course not. We are wired for goodness and happiness as descendants of the first man and woman, though sin has circumvented the wiring.

God's goodness and what He defines as good no longer satisfies. What does? Everyone's personal preference of good is a relative standard. Contrary to the one receiving a gift, the giver may think it is an excellent choice. Nibbling a bar of dark chocolate is one person's "Ahhh" moment on a very bad day. Another might say, "Yuck! Dark chocolate tastes terrible. I'll take a double salt caramel latte."

All happiness has a lifespan. With the last residue licked off her fingers, the chocolate lover sighs, "Mm, that was good." The latte drinker agrees as he tosses the empty paper cup into the trash.

After Adam and Eve's first bite of good and evil, good became tenuous in our lives. Decay exists around and in us. Because we are their sons and daughters, we are all too familiar with death. At the first hint of threat, we become warriors battling for the life of our good — our objects of affection. We turn to God. Or not. If we do, and He does not intervene, we wrestle with what we know.

"Where is God's goodness? Why does he not intervene?" We wonder.

Questioning is natural. The seed of suspicion that God is not good imbedded itself in the human soul that day long ago when Eve, then Adam, ignored God and listened to someone else. They succumbed to doubt and distrust in a perfectly happy place.

"Eve ... Eve ... "

A creature she had never seen before hung from the forbidden tree. Yellow pools rimmed with brown stared at her from lidless eyes.

"Did God really say, 'You must not eat from any tree in the garden?'" [5]

Eve stepped under the crown of the tree. Doubt's poison muddled her memory.

The creature's skin glistened with a sheen of gold and amethyst in the dappled light of leaf shadows and sunrise. A short walk away the trunk of the Tree of Life beamed in dawn's rosy flush.

She answered, "We may eat fruit from the trees in the garden, but God did say, 'You must not eat fruit from the tree that is in the middle of the garden, and you must not touch it, or you will die.'" [6]

"You will not certainly die," the serpent said to the woman. Fragrance from a morsel escaped its mouth. "For God knows that when you eat from it your eyes will be opened, and you will be like God, knowing good and evil." [7]

The serpent's misdirect of her Beloved's simple and protective instructions found its mark. She looked up into the arch of the grand tree, its branches heavy with fruit begging to be picked. The serpent swung to a lower branch rich with options at her eye level. Juice dribbled from his mouth onto her hand.

Eve took another step closer. Her eyes roved over the delicacies bobbing in a burst of wind. Their leaves swished past her arm; their breath tickled her skin. The earth's queen furrowed her forehead.

Surely the fruit was good. So, why would God not want her and Adam to know evil as well as good? Wouldn't it be wise for them to know what they didn't know? What was God withholding?

She wrapped her fingers around the perfection and tugged. With little resistance, it nestled in her palm. Her teeth sunk into the pulp laden with sweetness.

Mmm. Soooo good. Adam will love this!

Eve gave Adam the fruit, and he ate. Immediately they learned what "surely will die" meant. And there was nothing good about it. Innocence died. Knowledge of evil invaded them and all creation with a vengeance. Sin, a new DNA, impregnated the soul.

God's image shattered into a self-portrait of pride and defiance. Now the king and queen of the earth each ruled their own universe — the kingdom of self. A self-deserving appetite began directing their choices. The desire for God shriveled to a self-serving want.

A quandary loomed for Adam and Eve. God was coming for an evening stroll. They drowned in dread at the thought of meeting Him. Can you imagine the pressure?

Horrified because they were naked, they spent the day at the base of a fig tree stripping its leaves and twigs, fitting and sewing themselves a quick solution to their dilemma. Then they hid, but not with anticipation. Fear, not laughter, bound them in their hiding place. The moment arrived. Adam and Eve emerged throwing blame at God, one another, and the serpent. [8]

Genesis 5 underscores the consequence of their choice with "and he died" written eight times. The chapter documents the generations from Adam to Noah with the age of each father at the time of his heir's birth. Most lived into their 700s, 800s, and 900s. Life remained prolific, but death changed everything. Things were not as they had been in the Garden of Eden, nor could they be. That life perished with a simple willful act of disobedience. A new one began rife with pain and suffering.

All creation groans with death and mourns because of the separation between God and His beloved image. In his song, "Turn, Turn, Turn," Pete Seeger, a folk singer of the 1950-60s, popularized a 3000-year-old poem about death touching every goodness.

> There is a time for everything
> and a season for every activity under the heaven: a time to
> be born and a time to die. [9]

Every tangible and intangible goodness we experience in our lives dies. That is normal. When the marriage disintegrates, the career fades, the baby is born flawed, we grieve. The poem looks honestly at what cannot be avoided, but with hope.

> A time to weep and a time to laugh,
> A time to mourn and there is a time to dance.[10]

We have a name for a time to weep and a time to mourn. Grief — an uninvited but trustworthy companion that leads us to the goodness of God we lost in the Garden of Eden. There are two kinds of grief: before loss, and after.

Grief after loss is like a mountain buried in winter. Silence mourns among trees stripped of green. Cold devours life from leaf, stalk, and vine, leaving trees as statues in memoriam to summer. It is natural to cloak ourselves with denial and walk in loss with heads lowered against its pain as we trudge toward normal. We miss the gift of grief in our hurriedness, or our denial. We can learn something from the mountain where bright baby green will come, but not before autumn or winter.

I have had two life-changing losses. After the first loss, I did not know grief was a gift. My father died suddenly in the spring of my junior year in college. His body was donated to science so there was no funeral, no closure which people often find in a burial. My family gathered in a packed church with friends to rejoice Daddy's presence in heaven because of his personal faith in Jesus Christ. We sang hymns, read scriptures that declared this truth, and celebrated heaven.

Daddy's absence was our reality. A husband, father, friend was gone and there seemed to be no room to grieve our loss together. Our immediate family parted ways at the end of the weekend. My sister went to her family in Michigan, my brother to his home in proximity to my mother in Pennsylvania, and I to college in Florida. A heaviness I could not shake weighted my heart.

That summer I returned home and wondered if my mother ached as I did. While I worked on the children's staff at my church, the pastor discerned my depression as bottled grief. He gave me time in his presence each week to unpack what I had lost. He listened. He and his wife gave me a secure place in their home over many dinners to wrestle with pain, bewilderment, and the anger left in the bottomless sinkhole where Daddy had been.

Out of many conversations clarity emerged. Acknowledging the pain of my daddy's absence led me to cling to the certainty of God, my eternal Father who was always present. He would not abandon nor forsake me. As that summer ebbed into autumn, grief watered this unchanging truth. It cracked open and blossomed. When I returned to school, I could deeply inhale my loss like a sachet of summer's fragrance tucked away in bureau drawer.

The second life-changing loss began after Hannah's first-month checkup. Her pediatrician agreed with my mother-in-law. Something was wrong.

One month and two hospitals stays later Hannah's day nurse informed Coleman and me that a doctor—a specialist—and his team would be in sometime around 10 a.m. The large wall clock in the ICU nursery ticked ... and ticked ...

Silence hung between us. Our hearts ached in unison. We hoped this specialist had answers. He did.

Test results showed she had cystic fibrosis (CF), a genetic disease. Genetic? How could that be? Neither Coleman nor I had any history, nor any of the symptoms we saw in Hannah. Nor were we familiar with what he or his team told us would be coming in the future.

We expected solutions.

He didn't have one. The cause and diagnosis was, and still is, beyond the scope of human knowledge.

"The life expectancy is between nine and twelve years old, but the daily regime of care and going to scheduled follow-ups with a CF clinic can give Hannah life far beyond that."

Fear clutched our hearts and they cried in unison, "This is not good."

For nine months, we had prayed while God formed Hannah in secret. We reread again and again a description of Hannah's secret life only God knew:

For you created me in my inmost being;
You knit me together in my mother's womb.
I praise You for I am fearfully and wonderfully made
I know that full well.
My frame was not hidden from You in the secret place,
when I was woven together in the depths of the earth.
Your eyes saw my unformed body;
All the days ordained for me are written down in your
book before one of them came to be. [11]

We prayed, "May this child be knitted together in such a way that his or her life leads others to you. Thank you that all his or her days are interwoven in Your story."

From the day Coleman and I met, we heard a clear call to trust God with all our hearts even in times of mystery and confusion. We had inscribed the reference to Proverbs 3:5-6 in our wedding rings to remember no matter how old we became and no matter our circumstances, His trustworthiness remained unchanged.

We had trusted him implicitly. We never imagined where He would take us. He answered explicitly. The fight with CF began the day of diagnosis.

My heart beat with the pace of a lioness guarding her endangered cub. I would take the utmost care of this child.

The physical therapist showed us the thirty minute percussion therapy we would do twice a day every day to keep Hannah's lungs clear of sticky mucus. She placed a pillow over her thighs and knees, then lay Hannah upside down on it.

"The lower lungs drain to the bronchial tube against gravity, so it's important she lies upside down for the percussing of the lower six lobes."

She curved her right hand into a cup and raised her arm so we could see. "This is how you shape your hands to create a pocket of air." She put her left hand on Hannah's diapered torso to keep her secure.

A muffled steady beat began on Hannah's back. "Do this for two to three minutes on each lobe."

The "clap, clap, clap" continued. No one spoke. Hannah's eighteen and a half inches lay stretched and still.

"I'm surprised she doesn't cry," I said.

The therapist finished the back and turned Hannah on her right side. I could clearly see her face.

"Is she asleep?"

"Oh, that's not unusual. She's used to movement and being upside down."

The therapist covered Hannah's legs firmly with her right forearm and hand. Her left hand percussed the lower right side. The rhythmic beats syncopated with different machines in the room monitoring other babies' vital signs. With the bottom positions finished, she sat Hannah's newborn body against her chest. She leaned back so the head wouldn't slump forward unsupported. She thumped the right top front lobe, then the left.

"Make sure you do two minutes in each position when she wakes up, and at bedtime. This keeps mucus from building up in her lungs. If she starts getting a cold or teething, percussion three to four times a day. We want to avoid pneumonia, which can become the common cold for someone with CF."

Pneumonia? Coleman and I exchanged glances.

"The more infections," she switched hands. "The more scarring occurs and the airways become permanently blocked."

Our eyes locked. She leaned Hannah's chest forward in the crook of her arm to pillow the head. I envied Hannah's innocence.

Finished, the nurse cradled then carried her five pounds, six ounce body. Left hand under her head. Right hand under her torso. The nurse lowered her into the crib. Locked the side. Hannah settled on her stomach in a fetal pose. Her oblivion remained unbroken.

"Someone will be in about 4 p.m. for her treatment. I'll see you tomorrow."

"Thank you so much," we both said.

We took Hannah home ten days after the diagnosis and faced off with CF daily. Our days began and ended with administrating Hannah's breathing treatments and physical therapy. Every clap I made was a blow against the statistics against her.

Through the years, Coleman wanted to express his grief to me, but I could not listen. Though our hearts carried it in unison, sorrow lay silent between us.

Hannah lived twice as long as the doctors had first suggested. After her death at age twenty-four, Coleman and I learned that the grief we were living with was normal. It had a name, anticipatory grief. The grief before loss.

Medical diagnoses such as Hannah's are the most familiar types of anticipatory grief.

An MRI shows breast cancer metastasized into the lower back. A parent's forgetfulness slips into Alzheimer's. A two-year-old boy is riddled with leukemia.

Other life circumstances carry their own anticipatory grief. Conflict tears a marriage. Dialogue turns to divorce. The first foreclosure notice arrives in the mail.

Anticipatory grief is life on a mountain in autumn. The earth remembers and sighs with our ache for what once was. She tilts her head ever so slightly from the sun's embrace.

She whispers, "Remember and weep with me for what was lost in Eden."

Summer's green shivers and pales.

The sun remains constant. Radiant. He whispers back, "Remember and hope. Eternal goodness did not die in Eden. God has not left you alone."

A spectrum of browns shout from the mountaintop. The echo reverberates across valley and field. Vines shrivel. Cornstalks brittle. Empty milkweed pods tremor. The coming winter propels autumn's grace.

A mysterious transformation occurs. The mountain dresses in blazing yellows and brilliant reds with a dash of maroon and splashes of orange. Pumpkins dominate pies and porches. Apples and corn overflow autumn's basket. A different kind of life shimmers. Acorns fall like tears. The milkweed pod explodes. The wind snatches its life away. Locked in hard shells burrowed beneath decaying leaves, the hope of summer's green waits for spring.

In the autumn of loss, we wait.

The chill of a progressing disease or an appointment with the divorce lawyer place a layer of frost on hope.

We wait some more.

Each bright moment harvested, each morsel of good news, floods the heart with hope. Laughter bubbles from the deep.

Again, we wait.

Will the anticipated loss come? When will it come?

I lived with those questions on normal days during the CF journey with Hannah. Every time Hannah's cough intensified, fear erupted. Every time her weight dwindled, my mind scrambled for answers. Every time her energy diminished, my heart twisted.

My God, you could stop this. Have mercy.

Every time Hannah's lung function remained the same as the last CF clinic checkup, relief invaded. Every time the next checkup was more than three months, gratitude bubbled. Every time oral antibiotics, rather than IVs cleared infection, my heart laughed.

How good, good, good God is. How gracious.

Fear and hope keep vigil in anticipatory grief. We fear as we watch yellow tinge the green of our treasure. We inhale hope at the tiniest circumstance that contradicts or stalls its ebb.

In our autumn of loss, grief leads us to a better knowledge of God's eternal goodness. It is not the time to hide — to deny. It is time to weep and mourn. Not as victims, but as travelers in pain and suffering that began once upon a time in a garden named Eden.

God is more than familiar with our grief. He is the protagonist and hero of our grief story.

CHAPTER 3

What Does God Know About Grief?

My idea of God is not a divine idea. It has to be shattered time after time. He shatters it Himself. [12]
– C .S. Lewis –

"Adam, where are you?"

Four words of agony. God's beloved believed they could be like him without him. Oneness was rent in two. Them from Him.

But, God did not abandon Adam and Eve that fateful day, though it may seem so. Their friend became their judge. The gavel pounded and the sentence passed. They would now know limited goodness twisted with pain and suffering. Life would end in death. Relationships would be rife with conflict—with others and with the earth. Work, once effortless and joyous, would be grievous. The woman would know pain in childbirth.

The sentence was swift. He expelled them from their home and set angels with flaming swords at its gate.

God said, "The Man has become like one of Us, capable of knowing everything, ranging from good and evil. What if he now should reach out and take fruit from the Tree of Life and eat, and live forever? Never—this cannot happen!" [13]

This is not a vindictive God talking. Angry? Yes. Justified? Yes.

This was an irreconcilable lovers' quarrel. Adam and Eve had turned their faces and hearts from Him.

Death's eternal magnitude affected all creation from the grandest to the microscopic, visible and invisible. But God would not leave His image hopeless—forever divided from Him. He would deny the earth's king and queen another bite of the Tree of Life. His unconditional love cast them from Eden.

I wonder about, and can only imagine, the grief of the Lover of our souls. Did anger vibrate in God's voice and flash in His eyes as He voiced the curse of suffering to Adam, then Eve, and finally the serpent? Did He usher them to the gate of Paradise in silence? Did His heart twist with sorrow? Did He weep as the gate closed between Him and them? Before their expulsion, God replaced ill-fitting and scratchy fig leaf garments they had made with animal skins. His provision was more than a practical and durable upgrade. His action pictured what he would do many generations later. [14] Once and for all He would provide the remedy. Until then, the story of all love stories would continue unbroken. The lover would pursue the loveless.

A plan was in motion.

His hand spilled the blood and pierced the flesh of an unblemished substitute. Did tears cloud His vision as the knife plunged into the unblemished animal? Did His hands shake with grief as He covered Adam and Eve with its skin?

God created a simple hands-on metaphor of the consequence and remedy for His wayward lover. An innocent life for a guilty one. He made the first sacrifice, the first re-enactment of His solution to our sin problem. His pursuit of us has never wavered, nor can it. His love is jealous for what should be. Jealous? Yes. And justified. Humans are His image created for relationship with Him.

Sacrifice became a spiritual practice in Adam's household. One day Adam's two sons each brought an offering to God. Cain, the farmer, brought fruits of the soil. Abel, the shepherd, brought fat portions from some of the firstborn of his flock. God responded with favor on Abel's, but not on Cain's. His anger smoldered.

God asked, "Why are you angry? Why is your face downcast? If you do what is right, will you not be accepted? But, if you do not do what is right, sin is crouching at your door; it desires to have you, but you must rule over it." [15]

God's words ignited Cain's anger. He killed his brother, then went about his business.

"Where is Abel?" God asked.

"How should I know?" Cain shrugged, "He's not my responsibility."

"Cain, what have you done?" [16]

The question shakes with grief. Cain, like Adam, did not comprehend that God's unconditional love cannot deny his holiness. None of us do, for we are of Adam's race, conceived with a willful independence from God — a freedom for which we were not designed.

Cain's independent choice had consequences. He was expelled from the land he and Abel had made their home and became a restless wanderer. But God marked him in such a way "that no one who found him would kill him." [17] God's holiness did not, and does not, contradict His unconditional love and grief. His heart weeps as that of a father when his son foolishly goes his own way.

Ten generations passed. Society had become a sea of evil. Violence filled the earth and all creation suffered. Goodness was rare. God grieved. His heart broke for what once was. He decided to start fresh with Noah, a man who walked with God.

His story borders on being a fairy tale. He built a boat according to God's architectural blueprints in the middle of the desert for his family of eight, a pair of every creature on the planet, seven pairs of the animals He required for sacrifice, and seven pairs of every bird. [18]

After a year of mocking Noah as he built his monstrous boat, what did the neighbors think when all kinds of critters flew, crawled, ambled, or sprinted on their own to the ark for seven days? The roars, buzzing, caterwauls, shrieks, and grunts must have made conversation difficult between the ark builder, his wife, their three sons, and their wives directing animal traffic. How did this forerunner of a cruise liner hold all of them and enough supplies for a year? By one of the countless miracles that knit together the story of God with us.

Noah was 600 years old and two months old when God shut the door. When he and his sons pushed it open again, life poured down the plank and scattered. Eager animals itched to make homes with their new offspring. His first business was worship. He built an altar to God and sacrificed clean, as in acceptable to God, animals and birds. The aroma pleased God, but the devastation and its lasting effects on the earth grieved Him.

He said in His heart, "Never again will I curse the ground because of humans, even though every inclination of the human heart is evil from childhood. And never again will I destroy all living creatures, as I have done. As long as the earth endures, seedtime and harvest, cold and heat, summer and winter, day and night will never cease." [19]

Ten generations after Noah, God promised a son to a seventy-five-year old man and his barren wife. Twenty-five years later Abraham and Sarah had their miracle child, Isaac. One day, God told the old man to take a three-day journey to sacrifice his son on a mountain. They set off with a donkey burdened with food and firewood. His son, unaware of God's instructions, noticed the obvious.

"Where is the lamb, Father?" Isaac asked.

"God will provide, son," his father answered. [20]

When they arrived at the site, the two of them dug, carried and laid boulders. They collected kindling. Isaac still did not see a lamb. Perhaps Abraham looked around as well. No bleating mixed with the howl of the wind on the mountain. He turned to his son.

There is no record of argument between them but we can imagine the myriad of emotion and thoughts in both of them.

"Isaac, climb on the altar."

Forehead furrowed, his son did as he was told with deliberate steps. The rocks he and his dad had collected made a loose foundation for the wood. He stood in the center and surveyed the view for the sacrifice.

"Where is the lamb, Father?"

Or did Isaac already know?

Rope in his left hand, Abraham extended his right, "Give me your hands."

Abraham roped the hands and feet of the son God had promised—the son he had waited for twenty-five years. He gripped the knife. Raised it, poised to plunge. Did his tears bathe his beloved son's defenseless flesh? Did his hand shake with the sheer will of obedience?

A voice from heaven suspended the plunge.

"Abraham! Abraham!"

"Here I am," he replied.

"Do not lay a hand on your only son," God said.

Abraham heard bleating. In the thicket, he saw a ram caught by its horns. He went over, extricated the animal from its prison, and sacrificed it as a burnt offering instead of his son. [21]

Three generations later, Isaac's offspring moved to Egypt where they became a slave nation for over 400 hundred years. [22]

God freed them, but not until He sent ten plagues against Egypt. Some affected Goshen, the land where the slave nation lived, including the final plague, death. But God provided safety. He instructed Moses to tell each household to slaughter a year-old lamb or goat with no defects. Its blood was to be brushed on the sides and tops of the doorframe.

"The blood will be a sign for you on the houses where you are, and when I see the blood, I will pass over you. No destructive plague will touch you when I strike Egypt. " [23]

The scene of darkness and death dramatically pictures the universal plight of all humanity. The sin of Adam is genetic. Death of body and soul is our common destiny.

We decide what is good or evil for ourselves. We pursue our own happiness. We insist God do things our way, in our time. If He seems to ignore us, we wonder if He loves us. Yes, most definitely He does. The tenth plague in Egypt pictures how.

God added detail to the picture which began in Eden. God, the Judge, provides the means by which all can be saved. As it was for each household in Egypt and Goshen, so it is for each of us. Sacrifice after sacrifice, the picture is clear. We cannot save ourselves. When shall we be saved from death? Who shall it be?

In a fairy tale, that would be the prince dislodging the bite of poisoned apple with a kiss. Every fairy tale, ancient, classic, or modern, is a mere shadow of the true story of God's rescue of love. Thirty-four generations after God passed over each door trimmed in blood, our flesh-and-blood Prince left His kingdom, the place where everything is as it should be. His Father, the King watched as the Son descended. What was the goodbye like?

The Son entered the egg of Mary, a peasant virgin from Nazareth. Encased in the womb, He limited Himself to the mystery of being formed. God became flesh and blood. Nine months later a one-of-a-kind baby was born, Jesus of Nazareth. He crawled. Sucked His thumb. Stubbed His toe. Cried with pain. He ran in the street. Caught fireflies. Washed behind His ears, but never needed to ask God to cleanse His heart. No chasm lay between Father and Son. He did not sin.

Jesus knew loss and separation. Though He died years before His mother, it seems not before Joseph, His adopted father. Did He grieve when the man, who took Him to synagogue and taught Him the family trade, died? He constantly talked about His Father, His *Abba* (Daddy), in heaven. He often walked into the hills before sunrise, or snuck away on a busy day, to talk to Him just as Abel, Noah, Abraham, and Moses did. He prayed.

Jesus ate dinner, laughed, and slept in the homes of friends like Peter, and the siblings, Lazarus, Mary, and Martha. One day Lazarus became sick. The two sisters sent word to Jesus who was nearby. Surely He would come immediately to one He loved deeply? But while they watched the road and waited, Lazarus died. After the funeral and burial, a servant ran to Martha.

"I see Jesus and His friends walking toward the village," he told her.

Martha ran, gown flailing. She fell at His feet, grabbed His hands and sobbed. "Jesus! You...you could have... saved... Lazarus."

Yes, He could have, but He waited for a greater purpose: "I am the resurrection and the life. The one who believes in me will live, even though they die, and whoever lives by believing in me will never die. Do you believe this?" [24]

Imagine the murmur that went through the crowd grieving their loss.

"Did Jesus just say He was God?"

"Why does He make this all about Him? Why inflict pain on Mary and Martha?"

"Die, but still live? How can that be?"

Following Mary and Martha through the crowd of friends and mourners, Jesus faced the sealed tomb and wept. Why? His dominion over death, pain, and suffering had not diminished. Two other risings-from-the dead were on His resume. Yes, He wept as we weep when what we love dies. He did grieve the loss of His dear friend, but there is more.

His sorrow stretched the length of all time. He was the only human to know God's grief for what was lost in Eden. Our separation should not be. It is not death that divides us from Him, nor it's companions pain and suffering. The grief for our treasure is the fruit of the greatest grief of all.

Our sin is the chasm between us and our Beloved.

God no longer requires animal sacrifice since the last Passover Jesus shared with His twelve disciples. No more reenactment. His body broken, His blood poured out, the Son of God's life was the substitute for ours once and for all. When he hung on the cross, Jesus would know the full weight of our separation from God.

We can only imagine the details of Jesus' anticipatory grief before He died:

The Passover meal finished, Jesus and His eleven close friends walked to the Garden of Gethsemane, one of Jesus' favorite spots for evening prayers. This night His energy seemed spent at supper. He talked as if He gave final instructions.

They walked through the garden gate in clusters of twos and threes, but Jesus lagged behind. Each found a place to sit to reflect and pray. They had done this many times before. Often Jesus would plop down next to one of them, stretch out a leg, and lean an arm on the bent one. He would chat a few minutes, then amble off to the other side of the grove.

Tonight was different. He seemed restless as He stood in front of His three closest friends. Pain washed over His face. In unison, they jumped up. John put his arm around His shoulders.

"What is it?" Peter asked.

A faint smile passed over Jesus' lips, His eyes brightened. "You three..."

A deep sigh escaped Him. He rubbed His forehead. His eyes filled with tears. He squeezed them shut, and a few drops slid down the sides of His face.

"My soul is overwhelmed with sorrow to the point of death. Stay here and keep watch with me." [25]

"Sure. Absolutely."

The four walked farther into the garden while the others settled themselves against the stone wall at the gate. Their bits of conversation filtered into the night air and mingled with the sound of rustling leaves. The three settled on the ground around a squat trunk of an olive tree. Peter's legs sprawled in front of him. He plucked a twig to free a piece of lamb from his teeth.

He worked the meat loose as he watched Jesus walk away, "I think it will be a long night."

Finished with the twig, he tossed it. "Come on, let's pray."

Pulling his legs up, he wrapped his arms around his shins and rested his head on the kneecaps. Crickets hummed. The wind gently tousled his hair.

Without looking up he said, "I don't know about you, but I am *so* tired."

There was no answer. James and John were already asleep. Peter's prayers slipped into slumber. While they slept, their beloved teacher-friend knelt under another gnarled tree a stone's throw away.

Jesus begged His father, "If you are willing, take this cup from me..."

Yet He knew that was not Abba's will. This was the plan in motion since before creation. [26] He was the sacrifice pictured in the first slain animal in Eden, in Abel's offering, in the ark whose door Noah could not shut from the inside, in Isaac, in the lamb caught in the thicket, and in the Passover lamb. He was the Lamb of God who takes away the sin of the world. [27]

Now He lay prostrate, face in the dirt, "... yet not my will, but yours be done." [28]

The hours to His demise loomed in his imagination. Abba sent an angel to strengthen him, [29]though Heaven's messenger did not mitigate Jesus' anxiety. Blood dripped from His forehead like sweat into the sand.

At any time, Jesus could have freed himself from grief. He was God. But, He didn't. He was one of us.

Before the sun went down that day, God would be fully acquainted with our sorrow and grief.

Hours after His arrest in the garden, spikes pinned His palms to a cross beam and His feet to its support beam. Dehydrated and in dire need of blood, His life faded. The sinless suffered. Once again, He cried out, but not as God for His beloved Adam as he had done in Eden. This time as one of us.

Our sin, not His, rent oneness in two. Son was torn from the Father. Grief erupted between the two.

"My God, my God, why have you forsaken me?" [30]

And then, the eternal Son of God died. Jesus, who knew no sin, became sin for us. [31] The lovers' quarrel in Eden was reconciled. Forever. We need not be separated from God anymore, though it may seem so when what we love dies and He does not intervene. We taste our own sorrow unto death.

God's plan to come to us in our suffering instead of removing us does not seem a sane plan. Nevertheless, that is what He did, and does.

So You—God—know suffering
And cannot ignore our suffering
You came to the place where rust corrodes, thieves break
in and steal
Where bodies break, deteriorate, decay.
You suffered with us
You suffered for us. [32]

He entered our world with mercy's grace in His infant hands and returned to His Father with sorrow's grief scarred on them. From His long night in the Garden of Gethsemane, to His slow, asphyxiating crucifixion, Jesus experienced humanity's pain, fear, and despair. When He does not intervene in the early frost of our beloved gardens, though we beg, His eternal "Yes" to the deep and sacred work of grief transcends his "No."

CHAPTER 4

Things Are Not As They Were

"Will you come with me to the mountains?
It will hurt at first, until your feet are
hardened. Reality is harsh to the feet of
shadows. But will you come?" [33]
– C. S. Lewis –

Good grief. What an odd marriage of words.

I have used them a few times while driving, especially on road trips north to visit my mother who lived in Pennsylvania. On one such trip, I took interstates most of the way. Music on, cruising through the Shenandoah Valley on I-81, the miles fell away as I and my fellow drivers wove in and out of lanes toward our destinations. Suddenly, half a mile ahead, brake lights lit up across all four lanes. The driver in the semi next to me pulled hard on the brakes. They hissed, and I smelled rubber. Traffic filed into a single lane. An hour later, three miles down the road, we inched past two patrol cars and a car on the left shoulder of the highway. The driver and patrol men stood chatting. The dam burst, and the weaving resumed.

"Good grief," I muttered as I restarted the cruise control slightly above the speed limit.

Acknowledging grief as good seems counter intuitive. Isn't engaging grief a sign of weakness? An attitude of defeat? A lack of faith that declares God is good?

On the contrary, this companion that shadows us proves trustworthy on the journey of little losses. Its uninvited presence does not steal our happiness. Death does.

There is nothing wrong with embracing, caring, and celebrating objects of affection. Our delight is a fleeting shadow of the deep-abiding satisfaction lost in Eden. The DNA of God's life and goodness lives in every goodness we experience. Our hearts imbed their roots in the soil of our portions of goodness. The greater our affection the deeper the connection. The heart enlarges and beats with happiness. With eyes fixed on what we love, our hands grip our personal Eden, doing our best to keep them green. But when the shadow of death tinges green with yellow and our gardens blush brown, we cannot stop winter. How shall we prepare?

Anticipatory grief waits to navigate our trek on the mountain of losses in autumn.

How do we acquaint ourselves with this presence we normally associate with loss after death? We can first listen to those who assist others in their anticipatory grief journey, others such as Darlene Grantham, a nurse who specializes in palliative care for cancer patients.

"Anticipatory grieving involves mourning, coping, interaction, planning, and psychosocial reorganization. Anticipatory grieving is stimulated and begins in part due to the awareness of the impending loss of a loved one and the recognition of associated losses in the past, present and future." [34]

Unlike immediate death by a stroke or tragic accident, anticipatory grief includes what Darlene describes as "associated losses in the past, present, and future." These little losses happen like leaves falling in autumn. Over time, a fresh brown carpet covers the forest floor. The life of our object of affection can fade imperceptibly, and we manage the infinitesimal changes like the Energizer bunny, we keep going ... and going ... and going ... until the magnitude of loss weighs so great something urgent occurs.

Little losses mean subtle, significant, and defining changes. They uproot our understanding of normal. Their fingers seal the past. Things are not as they were.

"Beep ... Beep ... Beep ..." Sixteen months had passed since I had heard the sound of a heart monitor. Then, I was looking down at my scrawny, yellow-skinned daughter in a hospital crib. Now, tears obscured my view of her — my chubby-cheeked and curly-head cherub — as she finally slept.

Once diagnosed, Hannah's health blossomed thanks to a specialty formula and manufactured fat and protein enzymes. Malnutrition disappeared. Her lungs remained clear. Our daily habit of "percussing" twice a day remained a precautionary event in our normal day. CF appeared tamed.

Until today. Antibiotics dripped into her body through an IV stuck in her heel. The CF doctor's diagnosis earlier that morning iced my heart.

"The culture came back and it is positive for pseudomonas in her lungs. We will start IVs immediately. The physical therapist will be up to percuss Hannah once this afternoon and twice tonight. Every four hours. We'll continue this while she is in the hospital."

"How long will that be?" I asked.

"A course of IV therapy is about ten days to two weeks. Physical therapy will remain rigorous for the next few days. We'll adjust the schedule as we see improvement."

My hands gripped the crib bars. Tears leaked from my eyes and dripped onto the metal frame. For the last few days, her nose had been running clear. She fussed. Ate little. All were signs of two-year molars pushing through. But at daybreak, she woke crying with a fever and labored breathing. After a call to the CF doctor, we were in the car by 8:00 a.m. with orders to be at the clinic by 9:00 a.m.. Since then, Hannah had been poked and prodded. Nurses checked vitals in the office. Technicians took chest x-rays, swabbed her throat, drew blood, checked vitals, and searched for a vein to insert the IV needle.

Left alone and worn out, she slept. Or tried to. Intermittent coughs and big gulps of air interrupted her attempts to suck fiercely on her pacifier.

I rubbed her back and whispered, "Sweet Hannah, I am so sorry. Shhh ... shhh ..."

Things are not as they should be. Little losses crack, chip and shatter dreams and expectations. Things are not as they could be. They change plans.

I longed for my Hannah to share adulthood with me- to know the love of a husband and children as I did. But, as our normal life moved into her adolescence with CF, little losses clouded the vision.

At five she wanted to be a nurse like Grandma, who gave Hannah her nurse's cap. It would slip about her head like an oversized crown as she checked the lungs and stomach of her dolls with her stethoscope. But her dream changed at eight when her favorite home healthcare nurse gently reminded her, "You know, Hannah, being a nurse means being around germs."

Hannah's eyes widened. A shadow of disappointment crossed her face. The cap never came out of its box tucked on the top shelf in a corner of the closet. The stethoscope disappeared.

Eight-year-old girls should be able to play tag with the neighbor friends without doubling over in a coughing fit. But that was the year Hannah stopped running, withdrew from the swim team, and started piano lessons. Music was in her blood.

⋅A nineteen-year-old young lady who dreamed of becoming a musician should have enough air to coax a clear sound from her piccolo and flute. Hannah's lay tucked away in their cases, silent witnesses to CF's march on her lungs. During the second semester of Hannah's first year of college I wrote in my journal: "Hannah is slowly dying. I wonder where she will be in five years? " Her plan to be a worship leader shifted to finishing college — to finishing a semester — to staying infection free for a month — to waiting for a transplant.

Little losses shape an uncertain future. Things are not as they will be.

Coleman and I prayed for restoration each time an infection raged in Hannah's lungs. Others joined us as we pleaded for healing.

Perhaps there will be a day when one spouse will ask forgiveness and the other will give it, and their marriage heals - cancer will go into remission - the layoff or failed business will lead to a better job opportunity - researchers will discover a cure for diabetes, CF, Alzheimer's.

This is not the day. We pray that day is tomorrow, or the next day.

Even then, things will not be as they will be. One day "all will be well, and all manner of things shall be well." [35] The love story of all love stories will end with "and they live happily ever after." God will live among men. He will wipe away every tear. There will be no more death, crying, or pain. The old order of things will pass away. [36]

That is how things will be. But not today.

Layers of connection — memories, emotions, dreams and expectations — build a mountain of happiness where we each live with our object of affection. The sea of little losses imperceptibly erodes our secure foundation by days, weeks, months, or even years. Grief rumbles deep in the mountain. Winds of tension between loss and hope whip around its cliffs. The soil around the roots of our affection washes away. No matter how well we have loved, how well we have cared for our beloved objects, life wanes. Cracks widen. Chunks of the mountains slide into the sea.

Whatever normal becomes, the hope triplets, *could be, should be, will be,* always anticipate a better day tomorrow and strive for the best resolution. Always pushing, searching for a new angle or a fresh start, this kind of hope flings seeds of confidence where little losses have changed the familiar terrain. The wind increases. Some of the hope dies. Others grow tiny roots that cling to the mountain of happiness.

"Lap. Lap. Crash." Every day in anticipatory grief we watch little losses beat against our cherished goodness. Things are what they are.

September 2001

Hannah started college as a music major. Every school day I listened for the low hum of the aerosol machine that signaled Hannah was awake.

I would look at the clock. *Let me see. In fifty minutes I'll start her breakfast...*

It was a silent agreement between us made a few weeks into college life. She did her daily morning breathing treatment to open the airways and cover them with a mist of antibiotics, and "percussed" herself with the electronic vest designed to replace hand "percussing." When the rhythmic thumps of the vest ceased, and I heard the shower on, I would start her breakfast of eggs, bacon, and toast.

Every morning I watched my eighteen-year-old daughter, with a brush of make-up, in junior girl jeans, plod into the dining room as if a full day had come and gone. The will of a giant pushed her eighty-five pound body. I had offered to drive her to school so she didn't have to walk from the parking lot to class, but she declined. I understood. She was the proud owner of a red Taurus since high school graduation and a college student gaining her independence — as life should be.

"Thank you for breakfast," she said as she stood at the open front door adjusting the strap of her green book bag over her shoulder. She flicked her long, straightened curls away from her face with two fingers dressed with her high school ring and one shaped like a heart. Pewter silver earrings dangled from her ears. A silver Celtic cross hung around her neck.

She gave my shoulders a gentle squeeze goodbye. Her quick labored breath whispered in my ear. It haunted me, as if to say, "There is nothing you can do." I watched her walk to her car, leaning under her scholastic burden. It didn't seem right she should carry such heavy weight on her small-framed shoulders.

As she backed out of the driveway, I followed the car to the end of the driveway and watched the sedan puff down the street. When it rounded the corner, she honked. I waved and whispered, "Please, God, keep the germs away. Please protect Hannah."

I ambled back to the house, stopping to pull a weed or two, my calm exterior on display if any neighbors were watching. On the inside, I stood on top of my mountain and screamed to be heard over the roar of the ordinary, "What can I do? God, why do You not save her? Where are you?"

He is with us on the mountain in the fog of grief. He knows the unknown. He sees the erosion. God's is in the center of what things are.

> God is our refuge and strength,
> an ever-present help in trouble.
> Therefore we will not fear, though the earth give way
> and the mountains fall into the sea,
> though its waters roar and foam
> and the mountains quake with their surging. [37]

No matter what happens, how much normal changes or how deep the heart aches, we can trust God to lead us to rest in the mystery of His goodness as we stand helpless against the sea of little losses in thickening fog.

Trust when He says "No"? Yes. When He is silent? Yes.

But why should we trust God when He does not save our object of affection? How can He not intervene and still be good? We must remember, when all was as it should be in the Garden of Eden, eternity with God filled Adam's and Eve's hearts with happiness. Their enjoyment of other things came from a satisfied soul. We taste that "ahh" on our mountains. When Adam and Eve chose their own way, their contentment died in them and all their descendants, including you and me. His goodness pursues reviving in each of us what was lost in Eden—complete trust in Him. Especially when our mountain crashes into the sea.

Trust cannot be manufactured and put on like a piece of clothing. It is a seed formed in the autumn of loss. The shell softens in the fog and tiny roots attach to our hearts. Trust grows best in the rain of grief.

Jesus knows something about that. In the Garden of Gethsemane, God the Son anticipated His death. He pleaded. His body convulsed with grief.

Trust trembled, but held.

Jesus, the Man of Sorrows acquainted with grief, does not abandoned us in ours. [38] "No" and silence does not mean absence. Nor does the fog that cocoons us, forcing us to rest in mystery.

When

Things are not as they were
Things are not as they should be
Things are not as they could be
Things are not as they will be

Remember, grief's fog is normal. And good. It descends whenever and wherever—while picking up a new prescription for a stronger medication, setting the table with one less plate because he called again and won't be home, or waking up at the usual time and remembering there is no job to get to on time.

We must give ourselves permission to acknowledge the loss past, present, and future.

We can pause in the car, by the table, or lying in bed, and recognize grief with a simple statement. It begins with owning the emotion and ends with recognizing the little losses — what they were , what they will be, what they could be, what they should be:

"I am _____ because _____ is lost.

Things are not as they _____ because _____."

No matter how intense the erosion, how fierce the wind, or how thick the fog in an ordinary day, God is in the center of what they are.

The What of
Anticipatory Grief

Naked to rain
Beaten by sun
Tossed in the wind
Brown is undone

Supple to brittle
Whispers to sighs
Breath heaves little
Aching Brown lies [39]

CHAPTER 5

An Ordinary Day

Where there is sorrow, there is holy ground. [40]
– Oscar Wilde –

One day, I posted an invitation on my Facebook page while writing this book:

"YOU can be a part of my book on anticipatory grief. In the next two days, I'm looking for five women who are or have been in anticipatory grief (AG) — death slowly comes to something you love — your marriage, a job, a season of life, you or a loved one have a life-shortening disease. I want to share your stories of an ordinary day before and after you learned you would lose your treasure. I will describe your scenarios. If you are interested in participating, please message me. I will send you an email with two or three questions on it as the next step."

The following five stories are excerpts from well-articulated responses to these questions:

- What is the treasure you know (or knew) you will lose?
- What is (or was) your ordinary day like before that realization?
- How did (or does) your ordinary day change as your treasure slowly faded?

The women's willingness to share details and specific emotions reveals none of our stories of little losses are alike, but one common denominator connects them all — unrelenting stress in body, mind, and spirit.

Irmgard

"I was a typical 16-year-old in the Netherlands. Life was good. I had no worries, I partied with lots of friends, and was crazy about horses and boys.

"I loved and respected my parents, but didn't want to hang out with them. Being the youngest with seven cool brothers above me, they included me in their adventures. I was really happy.

"It was Tuesday, February 6, 1979. I rode my cool red Peugeot race bike to school dressed in a pink scarf, hat, and backpack. My friends joined me on the almost nine-mile ride. We always arrived early to school so we would have time to hang out.

"I didn't pay much attention to school. My only passions were art and math classes. The teachers were my favorites. That day my art class was cancelled because the teacher was ill. I decided to go home right away by myself. It was a beautiful, freezing-cold day. Blue skies. No clouds. I got home two hours early. Usually my mom was there when I arrived. We would have tea together. This time she wasn't, but I thought it was because I was early.

"I was reading the newspaper at the kitchen table when my brother's car drove up and two of them got out. It was strange to see them because they had day jobs and were not living at home anymore. It actually made me happy to see them. They were always up to something fun.

"That day, when my brothers entered the kitchen, and I saw their serious faces, a chill went down my backbone. They just hugged me and cried. I could not imagine what they were going to tell me.

"They told me my dad had died of a massive heart attack. He was with two of my brothers at his factory when it happened. They performed CPR till the ambulance arrived, but he passed away in the ambulance on the way to the hospital. I suffered memory loss because of the shock and I didn't permit myself to laugh for years."

Carrie

"I lost my treasured marriage. Once an ordinary day in my life would have looked like a beautiful family laughing, playing, joking ... My ordinary day significantly changed when my husband informed me we were divorcing. My world and my children's worlds were shattered. I hurt in places I didn't know could feel pain. My doctor said I was borderline risk for a stroke. I was made to feel unworthy of kindness, respect, love, or mercy ... a throw-away. I was replaceable."

Vickie

"Well ... my big treasure I will lose is my life, eventually. Before eight years ago, I took it for granted. At that time, I drove a school bus, but then I had an accident while driving it. Before that happened, I went to work, came home, and would do art without wearing myself out. I could go and do anything I wanted to do over the weekend with Chuck, my husband. I was a doer.

Not so much anymore. I have lost the ability to do what I want when I want. After the accident, I was in a lot of pain. The doctor prescribed physical therapy, but that made the pain worse. I chose the bus driver job because of the time off. The plan was to do art on my break in the middle of the day and during the summer and winter breaks. The last six months, on my breaks, all I could do was sleep, then drag myself back to work and finish the day. Weekends I was too exhausted to do much of anything.

It took almost a year before they found out I had tumors on my bones from breast cancer.

I thought I was going to be like my mom physically. She's always been a doer and a goer. I thought I was going to live a long healthy life. I had plans.

Soon after my diagnosis, I had surgery to put a rod and bolt in my leg. I went from a wheelchair to walker to cane, which I didn't give up. I just feel safe. I have aged *way* beyond eight years. Even though I have a 'disabled' parking pass, and receive disability from Social Security, saying I am disabled still feels strange."

Kathryn

"Mine was a long goodbye to my husband's mom. When she was 80, she made a courageous move to live near us. I was thrilled, because she and I had always had a loving relationship. Shortly after she moved, she had open heart surgery, and came through like a champ. The next seven years were a slow decline, but she was still active. At eighty-seven, she decided she no longer wanted care from a hospital. Then she was put on hospice because her heart was failing. What we thought would be a short stay in hospice ended up lasting two-and-a-half years.

Vivian—or Mammaw—lived next door to us. Every day I followed the brick sidewalk, which we had put in, to check on her after breakfast. I stayed for thirty minutes to an hour. I returned after her afternoon nap with her mail in hand. When John arrived home, we ate dinner, then went next door for another visit. I did her grocery shopping, met with the hospice nurse during her weekly visit, and met any other need Vivian had. Caring for her became a part of my normal rhythm of life. I lived in constant awareness of life and death, not knowing, each time I walked in her house, if I would find her alive or having flown to Jesus.

Even though she lived a short fifty steps away, I was haunted by the reality that she might die alone. Because of the love we shared, this was a haunting image for my heart to hold until a dear friend shared John 14 — a very familiar passage to me. In verse two, Jesus tells us His Father's house has many rooms, which He is preparing for us. I had skipped over verse three where He says, "if I go and prepare a place for you, I will come again and will take you to Myself." My heart leapt for joy. Even if I might not be there, Jesus Himself would escort her to her heavenly home. Vivian had become woven into the fabric of my day in the sweetest ways."

Sally

"I started each morning with him. With espresso in one hand, my other nested in his hand. We prayed as the sun broke over mountains visible from our living room.

"His initials, J.C., constantly reminded me of God, who loved me lavishly. He had placed J.C.'s strong, steady, sure arms around me. My husband quoted scripture while courting me. I had said we could not date for a year. This competent and vital, sexy, and strong man waited.

"He had already walked with God for sixty years. I could lean on him and learn matters of faith from him. We taught them to others. Together.

"We entertained. Our house was a gathering spot for God's people to pray, converse and laugh. J.C. drove the ski boat for his children and a hundred of their best friends. He greeted six grandchildren at birth, and cheered two generations at soccer, baseball, and basketball games. He applauded countless ballet and gymnastics performances, and kissed a thousand skinned knees.

"Once he called me from the ski slopes. He could not wait to come inside by the fire and share his exuberance.

"I treasured these moments — this man.

"Now, I listen. For his shuffle. When his footsteps become more choppy, I know he is about to fall. When do I grab hold of him? When do I yell, "stop!" How much do I shadow his every movement? I listen for the roll of his walker wheels. What has he slammed into? What corner has he caught? Has a rivet or nut broken loose that I will have to fix? He groans as he falls. I see panic in his eyes as I check for blood, or broken bones, or as I call 911 and direct the rescue team to the spot where he has landed.

"Once, he wrote me poetry. Now I read a few lines from a poem he wrote me six years ago. He says, ' That is beautiful. Who wrote that?' He sees my eyes moisten, then matches them with his tears. 'I can't believe I could have ever written that.'

"This man cannot remember why he can't remember. He can't remember what disease he has or what to do about it. Sometimes he calls me by his first wife's name, because he is in "the then," not now. My husband is a disappearing fragment, sometimes a sliver. One day, not a speck will remain."

These stories, poignant with love and loss, courageously paint pictures of shattered dreams, uncertainty, and emotional turmoil. Whether the wait is a few minutes, several months or many years, "constant awareness of life and death" in the "long good-bye" creates a climate of distress in an ordinary day.

The chronic tension that anticipatory grief creates was normal for me during Hannah's lifetime, though I was unaware until early one morning soon after she died. I sat alone in our sunroom. The fan hummed. Its breeze played with the edges of my journal. Calm invaded every molecule of my body. I leaned my head back and closed my eyes inhaling the peace. With the speed of a tornado, panic twisted my gut and rushed through my body. I sat up. My hands gripped the arms of the chair until it had passed. The unprovoked emotion was all too familiar. It had been my shadow on ordinary days with CF.

As days moved into weeks, then into months, the familiar turbulence of anxiety erupted in the calmest moments. Lying in bed between awake and asleep, or washing dishes, it would begin rumbling deep in the gut, explode in my throat, and cascade down my arms. I could do nothing but wait for the flood to subside. Now, years later, residual anxiety occasionally rumbles in stressful situations or without cause when I lie between sleep and awake. Something triggers memories of the daily battle.

But, now I know. When it happens, I take a slow deep breath and exhale at the same speed and fill my mind with thanksgiving that the Spirit of God intercedes.

Four months after Hannah died, I stood in the checkout aisle having just finished my weekly grocery shopping. My eyes glanced over the slick, colorful magazine covers. One in particular caused me to pause - an infographic of the brain on the cover of *Time*. [41]

I pulled the magazine from its holder and scanned the titles, stopping on "Six Ways to Handle Stress." [42]

I added the magazine to my purchases. After I had read, highlighted, and annotated that piece and a few others, I cut them out and pasted them in my journal. They, and other articles helped clarify my stress level and gave me much-needed permission to give myself grace. I was experiencing PTSD. Commonly associated with horrific experiences in war, the condition can occur after the death of our treasure. Grief is a distress. The little habits we use to acknowledge the losses before death, and our grief of them, will not negate grief after death or some level of PTSD. But, when the transition occurs, that grief can remain current and connected with the past. Not stuck in it.

Our bodies are wired to release distress, which is what occurs when a negative outcome is anticipated or will be at the end of a stressful situation. When we are in fear or are distressed, the adrenal glands produce and release high levels of the "stress" hormone cortisol. It should return to normal at the completion of a stressful task or event, but in unrelenting stressful circumstances the body revolts. "The hippocampus, the tiny part of our brain responsible for creating new memories and retrieving old ones, persuades the brain to turn off the stress response." [43] Cortisol levels malfunction as we fiercely fight for the life of our treasures. When wearied with combat, we seek escape in such things as comfort food. We watch or read mindless content, or isolate ourselves.

Adrenaline, another stress hormone, sends out a short-term "Danger!" cry for re-enforcements of strength, performance, and heightened awareness. In anticipatory grief, the danger zone widens with every little loss. For a family caregiver, the increased and unstoppable demands of more physical attention, more safety measures, more medications, continuously press multiple alert buttons. With no respite, distress rules the body and psyche. Tension mounts creating a spectrum of symptoms: burn-out, post-traumatic stress, stroke symptoms, heart attack symptoms, insomnia, excess glucose, irritability, and restlessness and others.

As little losses erode the mountains of our happiness, a good kind of stress does exist, and does invigorate. Eustress occurs when a positive outcome is anticipated in a stressful situation. Distress creates a fight-or-flight combat zone. Eustress rushes in to seize-the-day. It is often linked to a tangible goal. Planning a wedding, preparing for a new baby's arrival, or buying a new home, all promise a happy outcome, but each carry their share of stress.

Such tangible goals are monumental and life altering. So is anticipatory grief. These positive events require a major amount of concentration or commitment. So do the details that cause anticipatory grief. Instead of defusing distress, such goals can increase the daily pressure of the new normal. Any role that requires regular attendance, decision-making, or interaction compounds distress. Participation in such goals should be with little to no commitment, or, with an army of help. Eustress must be reserved as an outlet for distress to dissipate like toxic gas of a simmering volcano vanishing into the air. If that is not possible, resignation or a leave of absence from the position may be the next step.

Making small choices to slow down, we incorporate good stress in an ordinary day. Three types of eustress activities refresh the body, mind, and spirit: exercise, creative projects, and intentional relating.

A brisk, twenty to thirty minute walk or bike ride provides enough stress to increase the heart rate and blow oxygen through the brain. Bite-sized exercise can be woven through the day by parking the car a distance away from the entrance to the grocery store or climbing the stairs instead of riding the elevator. Inhaling and exhaling deeply and slowly while waiting for an appointment (especially a stressful one) or in moments of panic is another way to corral distress.

Creativity, an integral part of the human spirit, plays an invaluable role in an ordinary day between hope and loss. It is an action not a talent or a skill that brings something into being. It begins with doing something we love, like baking or letter-writing. Being creative can be as simple as interrupting a brisk walk to photograph a wild flower thriving in cracked concrete or capturing a tree's silhouette against storm clouds while walking to the car after a long day in the hospital. Sharing the image on social media breathes the small and simple bit of beauty and goodness through the internet.

The act of creating blows a fresh wind into the soul of a person in anticipatory grief. A simple chore such as making a pot of soup creates order in the chaos of little losses. While cruising through social media in a down moment, a new recipe may pop up that looks scrumptious. The process of collecting, preparing, and cooking the ingredients achieves a delicious result. When shared with a friend, eustress increases with an evening of laughter and levity.

Physical and mental exertion provide a reprieve from unrelenting distress. Whatever the exercise, it requires concentration in the moment. Mindless physical activity such as sorting, cleaning house, or gardening provide space for the mind to relax. Unsolicited but significant thoughts float to the surface. Their appearance, whether ugly or beautiful, help unravel what distress does to the soul. Writing those thoughts down (or recording them on the cell phone) puts flesh and bones to muddled emotions and perspective. They can be moments of clarity that breathe hope and eternal perspective into us after disappointing or difficult news.

The third eustress activity is the most challenging, complex, and takes the most energy—relating. Exercise fortifies the body and mind in distress. Creativity breathes life in the center of loss. But, relating provides an essential component to how we were made in God's image. He is a triune God in relationship. He designed us for a triad of relationships that supply much needed courage to engage with what we naturally desire to escape. Authenticity, in ourselves, with God, and toward others opens us to grief's trustworthy presence and reliable guidance.

Eustress activities expend energy and require effort. Often emotional exhaustion beckons a weary soul to escape from any kind of stress. A night's reprieve watching television whisks the imagination away and thankfully whittles away hours.

If absence from stress becomes an overriding goal, then escape becomes a habit and eventually a way of life. Addictions can form. Inactivity and carefully crafted isolation build cardboard dams against grief. The relentless waves of little losses flood the body, invade every crevice of the mind, drip into the heart, seeping deep into the soul. Grief does happen to us with or without us.

CHAPTER 6

Grief and Ourselves

The more faithfully you listen to the voice
within you the better you hear what is outside.
And only he who listens can speak. [44]
– Dag Hammerskold –

October 14, 2003

The day had finally come. My grief that Hannah was dying would not—could not—be ignored. I sat in a corner of a large room just off the elevators on the fifth floor east, the wing designated for CF patients waiting for transplant. Hannah had been on the list for a year. Her stable, 26 percent breathing capacity had plummeted. Infection raged. Her body burned with a fever of 105 degrees. My competent and conscientious Hannah lay bound in delirium.

I stayed by her bedside. Sat in a chair by day. Slept in it at night. On guard. Tuned for a hint of need. But, for once in her life, there was not a minutia of help I could give her. I was a shadow in the whirlwind to save her life.

This particular morning followed a very dark night. I curled up in a fetal position in an overstuffed chair. My eyes surveyed the large room designed as a brief getaway for patients and their visitors. A game table invited diversion in one corner. A big screen television hung on the opposite wall. In another corner, a bookcase stuffed with an eclectic assortment of books hid behind two overstuffed chairs. Their high wide backs built a wall of privacy. That is where I sat. Helpless. Scared. Alone.

Tears tumbled like a swollen stream in a thunderstorm onto the open blank pages of a new journal. Its first page held a small sketch I had drawn of a scene in gardens Coleman and I had visited a few weeks prior. The pen-and-ink drawing sat beside a handwritten excerpt from Lorica of St. Patrick's that began with, "I arise today through God's strength to pilot me." [45]

Little did I know how crucial the words would be.

In my solitude that morning, the years of packed anticipatory grief now lay exposed on the page. The grief I knew at diagnosis, carried through the years of little losses, and the grief I knew was coming, now lay exposed in verse. This metaphor for grief, "Brown Dances Down" that is printed in the introduction, inspired me to write this book.

This mother who fought fiercely for the life of her child could do nothing against a disease's vengeance. Without intervention, Hannah would die.

As little losses erode our outside world, grief presses and shakes the world within. Layers of the unspoken and unexpressed thicken and lie buried, unheard, unnoticed, untouched like an unexplored cave carved by an underground stream. Things as they were fossilize. Under the weight of loss and stress, layers crack. They may explode, showering whoever happens to be around in the most inane situations. They wonder, "Where did that came from?"

Grief will escape, whether we engage with it or not, like rivulets of an underground stream seeping from a mountain's rock face, or gush like a river falling off a cliff. It may not be tears, but anger or depression. Identifying grief's presence is a great challenge in the autumn of loss because we live in a conundrum. As long as death has not yet come, hope lives. At the smallest sign, eustress rushes through the heart lifting the spirit. Adrenaline pumps energy into the body. If we acknowledge little losses and the anticipated death, are we not giving up hope? Being morbid? Fatalistic?

No. To grieve well, a trust must form in three relationships: in ourselves, with God, toward others. The first step is to trust that grief is not the enemy. It is a gift from the Father of heavenly light, one for which we never ask or want. [46] Nor did Jesus who begged His Abba—His daddy—to make another way.

Trust leans not on the dubious gift but the Giver, who does not change like shifting shadows, unlike the fading of our treasures. [47]

Our first trust challenge is exploring our interior world. This requires time for intimacy with what happens inside us in the distress of the ordinary day. Coleman pronounces it "in-to-me-see," which succinctly defines its meaning.

Job, the man in Scripture of whom all patience is measured, paints a picture of the "into-me-see" journey into our interior world as he dialogues with his four friends from the ash heap where he mourns everything he has lost:

There is a mine for silver and a place where gold is refined
Iron is taken from the earth, and copper is smelted into ore.
Man puts an end to the darkness; he searches the farthest
recesses
for ore in the blackest darkness.
Far from where people dwell he cuts a shaft, in places
forgotten by the foot of man;
far from men he dangles and sways.

The earth, from which food comes, is transformed below as
by fire;
sapphires come from its rock, and its dust contains nuggets
of gold.
No bird of prey knows the hidden path, no falcon's eye has
seen it.
Proud beasts do not set foot on it, and no lion prowls there.
Man's hand assaults the flinty rock and lays bare the roots
of the mountain.
He tunnels through the rock; his eyes see all its treasures.
He searches the sources of the rivers and brings hidden
things to light. [48]

Paying attention to emotions and thoughts are like following
the hidden path, assaulting flinty rock at the surface, then cutting
the shaft to move deeper. As we busily go about our ordinary day, a
more significant life happens in the world within us. Discovering
what's beneath requires courage and patience. Dag Hammarskjöld
writes, "The longest journey is the journey inward." [49] Yes, it is, if
the destination is beyond knowing ourselves. Each of us is created
to love God and be known by Him. [50] That has not changed since
Adam and Eve. John Piper describes it this way, "What defines us
as Christians is not most profoundly that we have come to know
him but that he took note of us and made us his own." [51]

Grief leads in the way of humility, which is no well-trodden
path. With the light of courage blazing and the pick of honesty in
hand, we follow. The journey is a slow uncharted process. We
tunnel through thoughts difficult to confess and courageously
search the blackest darkness of our hearts not knowing what is
there. Dirt piles up slowly as the shaft deepens day after day. Grit
gets in our eyes and under our fingernails and blackens our face. As

Job alluded when he said no proud beast sets foot or lion prowls, facing what is inside reveals how thoroughly *humus*—of the earth— we are. It is no accident humble and human come from the same Latin root for earth … as in dirt.

The habit of journaling is a practice in humility. I have had many conversations with people who tell me they do not journal, all for the same reason: What if someone sees? Oh, what would they think if they really did know me? Fear echoes the actions of Adam and Eve petrified God would find them out when He came for His evening walk that tragic day in Eden. We, too, fear exposure—for we are ashamed when our flawed and sinful selves are naked, even to ourselves. I encourage journaling because this practice of humility gives us a place free of judgment. We are who we are. God already knows, and He has taken the judgment away. That is enough. Trust fortifies courage to defy that fear.

Write the date. Make an honest start. Like a miner digging through earthen debris, journaling begins with dumping what immediately come to the surface. What comes to mind? Is it something from yesterday? Anxiety about today? A dream?

If unaccustomed to journaling, begin with five minutes and build up to at least fifteen minutes a day. Writing implements are not assigned. Crayons and colored pencils are welcome. The pages can be lined or unlined. The parent-teacher-editor-critic that comfortably resides in our interior worlds is *not* invited to a "thriting" session. Journaling is not graded. To "thrite" is my made-up word that eliminated the space between "think" and "write" where my inner critic resided. No deletions necessary. No proper grammar required. No need to erase or start over.

As you write, watch for triggers, which usually indicate avoidance. These are the moments the pen pauses in mid-air or fingers poise over the keyboard. Sometimes there is a distraction, a random thought, a noise. Email, Facebook, or Instagram beckon. If that happens, do not let the parent-teacher-editor take over. If the mind goes blank, write the pause down: "My mind just went blank." or "I don't know what to say." Make dashes and dots. Doodle until something comes to mind. A new thought may interrupt. A detail about yesterday's appointment might be next. Keep making marks. Let them pile up on the pages. Do you think "thriting" a waste of time? Make that thought materialize. It is part of dirt in the interior world.

If something significant surfaces, such as unspoken stress or an untapped emotion, follow it. That moves the journaling deeper into the interior. Ask questions. Curiosity probes with questions like a miner uses a pick or an ax. There are no guarantees the lode will be discovered. Mining is the goal in journaling. Discoveries are gifts.

The goal of curiosity is not to get answers or to feel better but to become acquainted with the hidden world beneath your surface. Answers emerge eventually, and unexpectedly. "Why," "how," and "what" explore triggers. Questions such as:

Why did I react like that when ...?

How do I describe that feeling in my stomach?

Why do I feel like ... when ...?

How can "I-Me-My" questions be a habit of humility? They explore hidden motives, unbelief, and buried emotions that keep us from mining wisdom. "Thriting" helps pinpoint roots. I like to think of feelings and emotions as the nervous system of the soul. Unlike feelings that vacillate in circumstances with the unpredictability of a March wind, emotions lie deep and indicate the health of the soul.

They retain connection to life-changing events that effect current perception and relationships.

When interviewed about the movie *Inside Out*, Dacher Keltner, one of the psychologists consulted in its making, said, "emotions are the structure, the substance, of our interactions with other people ... Those scenes in particular with Riley's fights with parents and running away and coming back are all about sadness. That's what it really got right. Emotions shape how we relate to other people." [52]

Repetitive feelings of anger in our own lives can be signals of slumbering grief, an emotion. In the morning, a spark of anger ignites when a store doesn't open on time causing more stress in an already packed day. In the afternoon, a tirade pours into the phone at an automated message that blocks a conversation with an operator about unknown charges on a credit card bill. At bedtime, anger flashes because a toe just met the corner of a bureau and the pain shoots through the entire body. That repetitious anger has an emotional source worth exploring.

Anger and fear are common expressions in anticipatory grief, and grief after loss.

In rereading my journals written during Hannah's last ten years, I noticed a theme of anger expressed in various forms toward other people: jealousy, criticism, judgment (if naming a person in my journal I use one initial or a symbol). Here and there, I would write one-liners or brief paragraphs about Hannah fading. I was shocked I made little mention of her. How could that be? Saving my daughter was the warp of everyday life. Tnever left my mind or heart. Fear for her life burned white under my everyday involvement and leadership in ministry and homeschooling. But if grief was not part of my life-focused vocabulary, the absence made sense.

Grief showed up anyway, just not in the relationships it needed to.

Expressing feelings and emotions in collages or pictures articulate better than words. The best art teacher for visual journaling is a child. They have not learned to filter the nerve-endings of the soul. Therapists often ask children to draw a picture in family counseling to understand a child's perspective on family dynamics. A child draws symbolically, and so can we. For example, does anger rage? Red in western culture commonly symbolizes anger, as well as passion or love. Is anger monstrous? Grab a red crayon and write bold, big, angry letters across the page. A simple cartoon drawn with a straight-line mouth, wide "V" eyebrows, and little slits for eyes, easily symbolizes what churns inside. The animators of *Inside Out* did a remarkable job of picturing anger as a short stocky creature in classic red with heavy eyebrows and a head that exploded like a volcano.

Sometimes a journal is not enough to keep short accounts with the distress of the ordinary day. In time, consistent honest communication on its pages will show help is needed to unearth the upheaval inside. Signs of depression, for instance, can be rooted in suppressed grief. When these signs appear, seek counsel from a trusted friend, spiritual director/pastor, or counselor. None replace journaling and our conversations with God, but assist "in-to-me-see" with ourselves.

Our journey into our interior world, where we mine the ugly and the beautiful, does not end with finding wholeness for ourselves. Self-awareness is not of the greatest value. It is a just the beginning.

Job's journey of grief tells us there is more. By God's assessment to Satan, the god of evil, Job was the most righteous man on the earth. And he had everything: wealth, a large family. He was rich in notoriety, even with Satan, to whom God gave permission to strike everything Job had. In a few days, Job became familiar with destruction and death. There was no just cause for his loss of seven thousand sheep, three thousand camels, five hundred oxen, five hundred donkeys, all the servants who managed them, and his ten children. [53] Job's reaction? He worshipped God. He did not blame Him.

God permitted Satan to attack Job's body. He struck him with oozing sores that blackened his skin from heel to head. Job shook with fever. Pain screamed in his bones. Shards of pottery could not relieve the voracious itching.

His wife encouraged him to curse God and die.

Job chided, "Shall we accept good from God and not trouble?" [54]

Soon, grief descended with vengeance. He mourned his birth and the relationship he once had with God, saying, "How I long for the months gone by, for the days when God watched over me, when His lamp shone upon my head and by His light I walked through darkness! Oh, for the days when I was in my prime, when God's intimate friendship blessed my house." [55]

He ended his defense with his own character assessment. He searched his soul, and was satisfied. His evidence? He hid no secret sin, unlike Adam. His life's details and his reputation were blameless. No guilt hid in his heart. [56]

Job examined his life and found God wanting. He moved from embracing God's sovereignty to being discontented with God's lack of intervention in circumstances he believed he did not deserve.

Emptied of reason and argument, Job had nothing more to say. He had come to the end of familiarity with God and to the end of his knowledge and understanding—to the end of himself. That is a very hopeless place to be if there is nothing beyond or greater than ourselves. But, there is. The mother lode of wisdom can be discovered in the silence of our own understanding–in our grief where no answers shed light. God waits. Our darkness is as light to Him. [57]

We can imagine Him standing in front of us with arms open and hands beckoning. "Come."

He calls us by name. "In-to-me-see.
There is more to you, you cannot see,
because there is more of me you need to see.
Trust me."

CHAPTER 7

In-To-Me-See

*I don't think real spiritual maturity is
possible until you encounter the God who
appears to be insane. [58]*
– Dr. Larry Crabb –

October 26, 2003

Fever roared through Hannah's body, and she was lost in its storm. When would this particularly vicious fight with CF end. How would it end? Would infection consume her lungs? Would she live strapped to an iron lung? The doctor making rounds that morning said she might be, if the fever did not break soon.

Perhaps the doctor was exaggerating.

A tracing of a sycamore leaf rested in my lap. My journal perched on the wide arm of the blue, faux leather chair. An open makeup bag crammed with a stash of colored pencils and other art supplies sagged on the other arm. A few days before, I rescued the giant, brittle leaf, complete with holes and cracks from the bike path I walked everyday near the hospital. It now hid tucked between two pages in the back of the journal. The lines of its graphite replica stared up at me.

Hannah slept inclined, her face obscured by an oxygen mask. An IV needle protruded from the port on the upper left side of her chest that heaved in rhythm with her labored breathing. I sat in the alcove in front of the window willing the enemy to leave in the name of Jesus. The ding of call buttons and the murmur of voices wafted past the room.

I grabbed scissors from the bag. Their steel points marched around every line of the drawing. The great paper leaf fell dismembered in tiny shapes into my lap. I colored one canary yellow and glued it on the blank journal page—a no-name object lost on a rectangular sea.

What purpose, what meaning did it have now?

What was the purpose, the meaning of Hannah's suffering?

For ten days an army of antibiotics dripped into her veins like placebos. The round-the-clock regimen could not capture this fierce opponent.

The hope of a transplant teetered. Death — or an iron lung — loomed.

She tossed and moaned.

Why does God not save her?

Senseless scraps mounded in my lap. So many... like prayers...

I wrote on the right page of my journal, "Do prayers stack up like mail in your throne room? Do you just hear and nod like an old king who is growing senile? There is nothing miraculous happening here. Nothing — just more confusion. More battering. That's not true. Her white blood cell count is down, but for how long? Her respiratory rate and heart rate went down, but last night she felt terrible. Less junk in her lungs, but for how long?"

I grabbed the nameless bits of paper and sprinkled them around the glued, yellow piece. My understanding frayed, this was my picture of God right now.

Where are you, God?

"I AM here."

That's what God said to Moses when he wondered what credentials he would give to the enslaved Israelites as he announced he was leading them out of Egypt.

Who would believe an eighty-year-old exile from Egypt?

"I AM WHO I AM. This is what you are to say to the Israelites: 'I AM has sent me to you.'" [59]

"Who does God say He is?" I asked myself that day in the hospital room.

From the first chapter of Genesis to the last chapter of Revelation, God reveals Himself through a myriad of names that paint a picture of who He is.

I picked up a pencil and wrote "Alpha" on one scrap and "Omega" on another. [60]

You are the beginning and end of all things...the beginning and ending of Hannah's life.

I continued on: "Creator."

"God created"- the first two words of the Bible. [61] *You created her.*

I picked up another scrap and wrote "Life". [62]

You said that is who you are. You are the source of Hannah's life.

"Strong tower." [63] One less shape was empty.

The righteous run in and are safe.

Refuge. [64]

God, you are our help in trouble. And we are in trouble.

I penned "Potter". [65]

Yes, I still believe You formed Hannah in the womb with the cystic fibrosis gene. [66]

You could intervene. Why don't You stop CF's march?

"Sovereign" [67] came to mind and another piece was added to the pile.

And then another. "Truth." [68]

You cannot lie. You say You will never leave or forsake me. You will not leave Hannah.

"Healer." [69]

I believe the New Testament stories happened: the paralyzed man walked, the deaf man heard, the dead little girl rose from her bed. [70] Was my faith less than the blind man, the friends who brought their lame friend to Jesus, or Jairus, the little girl's daddy? Didn't I believe God was who He said He was?

Why do You not heal my Hannah?

I glued each shape marked with a name on the page with the yellow "I AM" speck, then drew a circle around all the pieces and colored the white space brown.

The "I AM" fragments floated in a brown sea — a picture of my fragmented faith.

Hannah's life dwindled.

Which would I choose? I could drown in grief, while clinging to the debris of a certain dream I had for Hannah, or I could rest on who God says He is in the sea of my grief.

Help me trust You are Yahweh, I AM WHO I AM.

Trust opposes suspicion, the predilection of the human soul. Oswald Chambers reminds us why we distrust Him. "The root of all sin is the suspicion that God is not good." [71] Our natural tendency began with our patriarch, Adam, when he and Eve doubted God had their well-being in mind. Why couldn't they eat of that tree? What was He with-holding? Curiosity led to distrust in God's word. Dissatisfied, they chose their own way. Physical death and its entourage of pain and suffering have permeated creation and our lives ever since.

We are all suspicious that God is not good regardless of how well we think we know Him, or how long we know Him. We may cling to what God says about Himself, but circumstances widen the distance between Him and our understanding. If it is not God's fault, whose fault is it? We turn inward. We wonder, "Why me?

Why my treasure? What did I (she, they ...) do to deserve this? This is not my (her) fault."

One day as they passed a blind man, Jesus' disciples asked Him if the man or his parents sinned. In the age of cyberspace and artificial intelligence, we still wonder whose fault it is. A sonogram in the second trimester reveals the good news. It is a boy! But, the images show abnormal development. A chromosome appears to be missing. He may die in the womb. His death could be in hours or days.

Good people are murdered. Defamation smears a person's integrity; costs him his job. A spiritual giant in her eighties loses her sight within days because of a rare eye disease. Why her? What did she do wrong?

Pain and loss descend indiscriminately because they are a part of evil. Jerry Sittser in A Grace Disguised describes our inescapable rendezvous with the pain of loss:

"It will not be denied and there is no escape from it. In the end denial, bargaining, binges, and anger are mere attempts to deflect what will eventually conquer us all. Pain will have its day because loss is undeniable and devastatingly real." [72]

Though an integral part of life, pain and death still surprise us. Inflict fear. Undermine our sense of well-being. We weigh pain against our own goodness. Either we think suffering undeserved or deserved and use fairness as measurement even for the pain of little losses.

Is it fair a child is born blind or with CF? Is it fair a faithful, loving spouse is spurned? No, but fairness is not the scale of goodness in the kingdom of heaven. When Jesus was asked the question about the man born blind He answered, "Neither this man or his parents sinned. This happened so that the work of God might be displayed in his life." [73] Blindness, the work of God? Or cystic fibrosis? Or ... you, my fellow pilgrim, fill in the blank.

What does "so that the work of God might be displayed in our lives" look like? Maybe that is not the question to ask. That is like a seed as it dies requiring a look into the future at the mature plant — the purpose of its death. Trust does not require we see the meaning or the outcome of what God says but accept His impeccable, eternal goodness — *love*. Trust slips its toddler's hands into Daddy's when he says, "Hold my hand."

What if instead of asking "why", "how", and "what", we ask "who" is at the center of our grief? Is it us with our tenacious demands that "I AM" be what we want Him to be? Or is it God, calling us deeper into that parent/child relationship with Him? Whether we believe or not, God made us to be in an "in-to-me-see" relationship with Him. All things in our lives are subject to that purpose. Darrell Johnson in *Experiencing the Trinity* writes, "God is intent on drawing near to us in such a way as to draw us near to Himself within the circle of knowing Himself, Father, Son, and Spirit." [74]

Pain awakens our ache for God's good that is unaffected by evil, for His love in our pain, for His wholeness in our brokenness. Our fallible and finite stories do not mar His eternal one. On the contrary, they are its flesh and blood.

Engaging with grief in the journey of little losses deepens or destroys our "in-to-me-see" relationship with God for which we are designed. Which direction we choose depends on how ruthlessly we trust. Once long ago for a very short time, God's image trusted Him implicitly, but there was no pain, suffering, or death. God promises no more tears, death, pain, or grief in an unknown but definite future. [75] But, in this in-between time, a relationship of trust with God includes all of them. C.S.Lewis writes in *The Problem of Pain*, "God whispers to us in our pleasures, speaks to us in our conscience, but shouts in our pains: it is His megaphone to rouse a deaf world." [76]

The Arctic winds will in time frost the summer green of our beloved treasure. We cannot stop leaves from turning brown. But we can engage with grief so that we are led to the one thing that matters forever — the "in-to-me-see" relationship with God the Father.

The Gospels, the four records of God's human life, give a composite of what we need to know about His "in-to-me-see" with us. The portrait Matthew, Mark, Luke, and John create gives us enough to see He is God and Man. Matthew, an eyewitness, begins by calling Him "the Messiah"—the promised One—"son of David," "son of Abraham." [77] Luke traces His genealogy from Joseph all the back to Adam. Mark begins his account with "The beginning of the good news about Jesus the Messiah, the Son of God." [78] John starts his biography acknowledging Jesus was with God before the foundation of the world. He identifies Him as "Creator" and "Life, which is Light of all men." Then, he writes, "And the Word became flesh and dwelt among us, and we have seen His glory, glory as of the only Son begotten of the Father, full of grace and truth." [79]

The details in the composite the four writers paint display Jesus living the human experience from conception to death. The narrations show His familiarity with our every weakness: prejudice, misunderstanding, rejection, death of a loved one, persecution, abuse, abandonment, physical suffering, loneliness, and more. But in His response, He did not sin. What does that matter in grief? Everything.

We cannot say God does not know what we experience. We cannot say He does not care, or understand. Nor can we say He requires we clean ourselves up before coming to Him. The sovereign and good hand of God that killed the innocent animal in the Garden of Eden, who provided the lamb in the thicket for Abraham, whose Angel of Death passed over every household in Egypt where an unblemished lamb's blood covered the front door's posts and lintel, did not lift a finger when His Son died for the sin of the world.

He was resurrected, returned to His Father, and now sits at His right hand. The Father and Son sit side by side on the throne of grace. We can boldly come as we are, as many times as we need to. Mercy and grace are available in the autumn of loss, our time of need. [80]

What is it we need in anticipatory grief? Strength of devotion in a trustworthy God. When layers of day-to-day emotional pain and the weight of a questionable future press down on every side, a deep work occurs in us. "In-to-me-see" with Him is not the same as Cinderella's relationship to her fairy godmother. On the contrary, knowing Him and being known by Him is a silent ongoing work like the transformation of years and years of fallen flora sinking deeper in to the depths of the earth's crust.

The strip mine looks like the ruins of a Greek amphitheater sunk into the earth. Its tiers of soft rock descend to a flat floor below. Syncopated clinks of metal on rock rise from the lower levels instead of the voices of orators. A dump truck the size of a thumbnail roars as it begins its climb. Its polished steel stack exhales a stream of smoke. With the speed of a snail, the beast of burden ascends carrying tons of dirt and rock. At the surface the air brakes heave a deep sigh. The truck sheds its load of graphite that will become charcoal briquettes or No.2 pencils, among many other ordinary things.

Organic matter dies year after year. Layers of carbon accumulate century after century into the crust of the earth. The deeper the layers, the heavier the pressure. They solidify into coal beneath and graphite on top. When hard-pressed on every side by the intense trauma of volcanic activity, carbon experiences a metamorphic mystery. Its DNA transforms. Crystalized but not crushed, the simple structure transforms to a complex one. Not destroyed, it can grow into crystals the size of soccer ball or melon. The death of graphite is the life of the diamond, highly prized and priced.

When stresses compound in one ordinary day, and when that day compounds into weeks, months, years accumulating layers of little losses, we do become hard-pressed with emotional and mental distress. Our interior world twist with perplexity. Plans and dreams are struck down. We feel persecuted. Deeper still - what we think is a rock-solid faith, melts. A metamorphosis shapes our character.

God says to us, "Do not despair. I do not. I am making a new creature out of you. I can mine limestone, but I shall wait until it is marble. I can mine shale, but I desire slate. Deep under your surface, my pursuit of intimacy with you shall heat your heart and consume your mind. You will not be destroyed, though this upheaval may feel like it. Out of your darkness comes my gold, jasper, and topaz. Sapphire and amethyst shall cluster with jacinth and chrysotile. Trust me."

Trust God ...

What does it not look like?

It is not the absence of questions but asking them.

It is not the absence of fear or doubt, or grief, but expressing them.

It is not feeling God, but clinging to who He says He is,

Regardless of how we feel, or what we think

Even if it means we cling to only one truth He says about Himself, I AM.

Trust is not complicated. It does not need to understand or be understood. It does not need to be in control, demand answers, or fear. Trust grips what creation declares is true.

The endless waves running down the beach morning, noon, and night sing, "He is the same yesterday, today, and forever."

The mockingbird calls in the morning, "Whatever happens today, He is."

At dusk the sun whispers, "He will not forsake you," as it slips beneath the horizon.

At dawn the sun beams, "He is the light of the world."

The drenched wildflower sways violently in the afternoon thunderstorm. Its parched roots drink eagerly, "Look! Don't worry. See? He provides."

In our grief, God the Father treats us as if the only DNA that matters in us is His, through Christ Jesus, His only begotten Son. As He should. Being transformed into His image by the Spirit is the only thing that does matter.

Grief opens the sleeping wound that suspicion has carved in the soul. The excruciating pain is not the enemy. We must not be afraid to follow grief into our interior world and discover the truth about ourselves and God, who meets us where we are in the heat and pressure of our distress. Dr. Larry Crabb describes it well in his book *Soul Talk*. "If you are a follower of Jesus ...

> The unconditional love of the Father
> The indescribable grace of the Son
> The infinite patience of the Spirit
> All, at this precise moment
> Live in the center of your soul." [81]

If a person is not a follower of Jesus, the invitation to the throne is extended. God waits in the heights of happiness and in the depths of grief. There is no need for us to clean up. The promise has no exceptions. Grace and mercy are available to everyone who choose to believe.

Whatever the circumstance of anticipatory grief, be assured in the chill of winter, God-life blooms in us and through us as our treasure fades. God does not judge grief but makes it His servant to lead us deeper into Him. Our trust in Him tells His good story to those around us. The presence of others is His tender kiss of love to us.

CHAPTER 8

The Gift of With-ness

*I am heartbroken for those whose lives are on
pause as the "beat goes on" for the rest of the world.
Raw grief is visceral. May those who are
'God here' come alongside to serve,
help, and pray.* [82]
– Wanda Rogers –

West Memphis, Arkansas, 1988

I stood in the kitchen of a couple who had been our neighbors in Wilmington, DE during those tense months after Hannah's birth. The wife had watched me percussion Hannah in our apartment. Her eighteen-month-old son played, ate, and napped with Hannah there on days she taught music in a private school. Hannah was a healthy, chubby, two-year old when they moved to Memphis. Six years later, we stayed with them over the weekend. A church was interviewing Coleman for a staff position, which included meeting his family.

She and I were catching up while our pairs of children chattered and chased one another through their two-bedroom bungalow. Our husbands were off to seminary. Hers was a student, mine a potential one.

"Wow, Hannah looks great," she said, "Do you still percussion her?"

"Oh, yes. That will never stop."

"Can you ever go away?"

"Go away?" I laughed. "That's not really possible unless there is someone who knows how to percussion. One of Hannah's nurses at

Children's Hospital, who goes to my mom's church, volunteered when her Sunday School class gifted us with a weekend away soon after Hannah was diagnosed. My mom has done it once or twice."

"Will you teach me how to percussion? I want to know what it's like. And, if you and Coleman come here to seminary, I want to give you a break. I want to be here for you; take care of your kids. You can be worry free."

The words sunk into my heart like rain on a wilting flower.

When we did move to Memphis, she learned the "beat." On days Hannah stayed with her, my weighted heart sighed with relief.

Relationships naturally grow out of normal days and shared interests. Friendship sings like a chorus of birds waking on a summer's day when lives intertwine. Beliefs and interests synch. In Wilmington and Memphis, my friend and I lived in proximity. Our families hunkered down with our babies in a snow storm. We moved easily through a routine. We shared a dedication to ministry.

The autumn of loss has its own rhythm. At first news, its voice whispers like the muffled hit of a mallet on a kettle drum. We know without a fight, death will take our treasure. Gradually the deep voice grows insistent. Its wildness breaks from the rhythmic tune. The erratic beats of hope and loss interrupt the steady beat of normalcy to which we are accustomed.

We cannot expect others to be attuned to our season or assume they are aware of its emotional syncopation. Fighting death is not a part of everyday life. Nor is grief. People who naturally follow normalcy's beat move away from us, like migratory birds who leave the woods for a warmer climate

Those who take the time to enter our world, give us the gift of "with-ness," the sweet taste of "in-to-me-see" in human relationship, like my friend who helped carry my load. The ache to be known intensifies whenever loss changes our lives. We long for our voice to be heard, but wonder who we can trust. We long for others to fall into step with the erratic beat. "With-ness" will come in random moments and unexpected ways.

"With-ness" asks questions that tell us we are noticed.

Life goes on, and we, who travel through our autumn, long for a certain someone—or anyone— in our every-day-life-community to stop midstream and ask, "How are you?" over the phone or coffee, and mean it.

Those who ask, like my friend in Memphis, want to understand our journey and join us in some fashion. After five years, she remembered the daily therapy that was part of saving Hannah's life. She wondered if anyone gave me respite from the daily battle.

My heart heard in her offer, "I imagine fighting everyday must be wearisome."

Caught up in their rhythm, people are unaware. Behind the scrimshaw of daily life, a woman fights to save a marriage or struggles to care well for her autistic child. If they do wonder, people can only imagine the tension of hope and loss, since they cannot see into another's interior world. They can only assume how we feel and what we need. Unless they, too, have experienced or presently live in a similar situation. Even then, they do not know our journey. Many people are afraid to ask questions and remain clueless unless we voluntarily inform them.

"With-ness" asks questions it is not eager to fix, but holds the answers of a burdened heart with extreme care. Some inquire, as my friend did, in order to best equip themselves to be a companion. Some use answers as fodder for gossip. Others think they have answers oblivious to questions they should be asking, like "How are you?" They offer their success stories as a universal solution—a hope that fits all.

Regardless of why a person asks or how they treat our "in-to-me-see," our answers can always be laced with humility and gratitude. Such qualities are not feelings but choices. With a smile and eye contact, a hug, or a handshake we can say, "Thank you for asking." Or, "You are so kind. Thank you for your concern."

Grief before loss is just as sacred as after, but it is unfamiliar. Too often people in normalcy do not know what to ask or are afraid of offending, so they ask nothing.

Some avoid asking. "That could be me," lodges deep inside.

Yes - it could, and will be. When it is their turn, we must remember that listening is at the core of "with-ness."

"With-ness" gives us space to grieve.

Job's troubles increased. Boils festered from his head to feet. Crazed by their fire, he scraped his skin with broken pieces of pottery. A trio of friends heard of his peril and agreed to meet at a designated place. They lived a few days camel ride from one another. Perhaps the four of them met once a year in a town equidistant from their homes.

We can imagine the details of this true story left silent between the lines of Scripture. What was their plan? Go, sympathize, and comfort the greatest man among all the people in the East? What did they expect? They just knew their friend needed them. Maybe— just in case—maybe they packed mourning apparel and prepared words of honor to say at his funeral.

Did they wonder at the state of mind of the most righteous man in all the earth? On the camel ride across the desert, did each imagine themselves in his sandals? When they slid off their perches to camp for the night in the desert, did they discuss over dinner why this happened?

We can only imagine their first sight of him. His nakedness wept with festering sores. His body ballooned with inflammation. He writhed with pain's tenacious bite in the sub-dermal tissue. Weariness tortured him. Suffering held him captive.

His friends dismounted. And mourned. Each tore the covering from his head and ripped his outer robes. The shreds fell to the earth, innocent reminders of what once was Job's life. Grief turned their knees to lead, and they sank into the sand.

How did they express their grief? That, too, we can imagine. Each man would have responded differently. Elihaz swung like a pendulum. Zophar bent like a fetus shivering. Bildad knelt like a faithful dam cracking under pressure. Tears seeped from his eyes clinging to the eastern horizon.

Sorrow crumbled their restraint. A trio of wails floated over the ash heap and dissipated among the whispers and conjecture of their entourage and Job's neighbors. With handfuls of dirt, the three showered their heads. Dirtied and torn they joined their broken friend on the trash heap for seven days. No one said a word to him, because they saw how great was his suffering. [83]

Job's friends gave him what many people think is useless or impractical. They gave wordless "with-ness" —like a company of musicians whose fingers rest on silent instruments, but stay attuned.

We have no record of what Job did during that time, but in his condition, I doubt he was calm, cool, and collected. Miserable, mumbling, and mourning would be more like it. Their companionable quiet stirred hope in Job. His dear friends saw him at his physical and emotional worst, and stayed. So, he entrusted his deepest anguish to them.

He confessed, "I wish I had never been born.

"With-ness" can fail.

Grief, our faithful companion, searches for another soul to share the ache. That is part of the human design. God did not create us to be alone. No matter how strong relationships appear, and have proven unshakable in the past, endurance remains undetermined until we risk exposure. The deeper the invitation "in-to-me-see," the more another person experiences our dirtiness.

Job's declaration on the ash heap after seven days of silence seemed so unlike him.

Did his friends look at one another with eyebrows raised? Was this the most righteous man in the east speaking?

When Job's filthy truth spewed over his friends, they reacted. Elihaz answered Job with the voice of wisdom by saying a person should not despise God's discipline. He corrects to build character.[84]

"Dear friend," he says, "If you apply these certain principles to your life, God will listen."

Bildad blames Job's troubles on his sin and his children's death on their sin. He encourages Job to look to the traditions of his ancestors for answers. [85]

"You know, Job, I am sorry to say this. God does punish disobedience. Do you remember what our pastor told us about appealing to God's mercy?"

Zophar tells him to do the right thing — be more devout, put away his sin, guard against all evil in his home.

"I promise you, Job, if you do those things, God will bless you."[86]

His friends' long speeches do not reach Job's anguished soul.

Twenty-first century responses gained from experience are not very different. They share "When that happens to me...," or preach "Let me read you a powerful scripture God gave me when..." or advise: "You know you really should ... "

"Don't you worry. God is good. This will turn out okay."

"When life gives you lemons, make lemonade."

None of these appease a broken soul.

Why do people deflect grief with answers, assurances, and suggestions? Or, react in anger or comedic relief? Some ache to fix the unfixable because they love those who hurt. Others see weak faith or flawed character and fear retribution.

They may fear to face grief themselves, like me when my husband wanted to voice his sorrow in Hannah's childhood. The warrior, who daily fights against the prognosis of potential death of their beloved treasure, thinks they cannot afford to grieve. Acknowledging grief feels counter intuitive to the fight for life or like a betrayal against the sovereign good God. Naming it appears to be a confession of defeat—a lack of faith.

Anticipatory grief is what it is - painful to feel, painful to witness, and a real and natural emotion that gives the soul a voice to say, "This should not be." Even the most righteous, the best person we know, will come to the end of themselves in the agony of grief.

A listener's silence responds, "I know. There are no words to make it better."

"With-ness" sees and attends to basic and ordinary needs without fanfare.

Gainesville, FL 2001

"We need to raise thirty-thousand dollars in addition to health insurance, *and* apply for Medicare?"

"That's right," the woman in the finance office nodded. "You just never know what costs are included in a double lung transplant."

Coleman and I left her office, hope drained from our hearts.

Where in the world do we get that kind of money?

A few weeks later we sat in another office. Our tax return file lay in front of our accountant.

"Good to see you. How are the Pratts?" he leaned back in his chair, hands behind his head.

"Well, we have some big news. Hannah needs a transplant. If she meets the medical criteria and we satisfy the financial requirements, she will be listed."

He leaned forward. "How much money is required?" His folded hands rested on the large round table between us.

"Thirty-thousand dollars."

He leaned back in his chair. His hands, still folded, fell in his lap. "Yes. That is a lot of money."

We finished our business, stood, and said our goodbyes.

He shook our hands. "I certainly will be praying about Hannah. God will provide."

One day in August an envelope with an unfamiliar return address arrived tucked among fourth class mail and bills. I ripped the flap and pulled out a business letter informing us our accountant had opened a non-profit account, The Hannah Pratt Cystic Fibrosis Foundation, with the required start-up amount, one thousand dollars. By December, 2002, the generosity of family, friends, and strangers met the balance of the required thirty-thousand dollars.

Not one penny paid medical costs. The fund covered expenses for Hannah and me while we lived in Gainesville from January 2005 to April 2006 and living expenses during the forty-four days after transplant. Monetary gifts given after Hannah's death were added to the unused amount. The balance was distributed to others with CF who were in financial need.

"With-ness" extends compassion without expecting recognition.

Gainesville, FL. October, 2003

One night during weeks fighting pneumonia, Hannah lay delirious. The night nurse became our warrior while I slept in the sleeper-chair. She had come in around midnight. I was up, holding my daughter's hand, who muttered and tossed.

She leaned down. Her words inches into my ear, "Hello, I'll be taking care of Hannah tonight."

I looked up and nodded. She looked a few years older than Hannah.

Each time I woke through the night to check on Hannah, she was there. Bathing her patient's forehead with a cool wet cloth, dampening her parched lips, readjusting the cooling blanket when Hannah's restlessness pushed it from under her body. When I wakened at 6:00a.m., Hannah's peer sat silently on the other side of the bed patting my daughter's hand.

The young woman's vigil told this mother, "You are not alone. I am in the battle with you."

"With-ness "can disappoint

Regardless of why, some will distance themselves instead of leaning into our circumstances and our grief. Some immediately. Others, like Job's friends, reach their limit later. Closeness may never be the same simply because one moves forward in normalcy. The autumn of loss changes the other. Eventually the two may move in different circles.

How natural to expect our existing community to be enough. The heart relies on such a friend through changes. We anticipate what has proven true in the past will be solid in the present. The deeper "in-to-me-see" in a relationship, the stronger the expectation. When absence replaces presence, the heart is dissed and emotional loss occurs.

"This should not be," the heart says.

It is what it is. We travel a different road then those in our former normalcy.

We are unaware our love for another transforms to demand until their "with-ness" fails. The interior world rumbles with a myriad of emotion - abandonment, bitterness, and anger, exposing entitlement in the heart. Regardless of how or why we are let down, what we think and feel is our property. The disappointment is a not-so-little loss in our autumn. Another green leaf from our summer has blushed brown. Broken from stem, it has danced to the ground. Smeared. No longer beautiful.

In our interior world, compounded emotions churn like molten rock in the crust of the earth. Grief can harden into cynicism, levied aloofness, sarcasm, criticism. But it can also form the gem of forgiveness.

It all depends on what we let live within us.

Corrie Ten Boom, a survivor of the Ravensbruck concentration camp in World War II, experienced that choice after the war. Her sister, Betsie, died imprisoned, too weak to sustain the hard labor and cruelty by the guards. While traveling through Germany teaching forgiveness, Corrie came face-to-face with one of their captors. At the end of her talk, all had left but him. He did not remember her among thousands, but her imagination flew to her sister's frail nakedness and his cruel face and leather crop swinging from his belt.

He put out his hand and identified himself as an abusive guard in the camp, "I know Christ has forgiven me. Will you?"

Corrie writes, "... forgiveness is not an emotion—I knew that, too. Forgiveness is an act of the will, and the will can function regardless of the temperature of the heart. 'Jesus, help me,' I prayed silently. 'I can lift my hand. I can do that much. You supply the feeling.'" [87]

That day she experienced "with-ness" of soul with her former enemy. She let vengeance and pride die. Sometime later, good friends, who shared her faith, betrayed her. She wrestled nights with the hurt. Had she not learned forgiveness? God gave her more understanding through a pastor to whom she confessed her failure. In *Tramp for the Lord* she writes,

> *"'Up in that church tower,' he said, nodding out the window, 'is a bell which is rung by pulling on a rope. But you know what? After the sexton lets go of the rope, the bell keeps on swinging. First ding then dong. Slower and slower until there's a final dong and it stops. I believe the same thing is true of forgiveness. When we forgive someone, we take our hand off the rope. But if we've been tugging at our grievances for a long time, we mustn't be surprised if the old angry thoughts keep coming for a while. They're just the ding-dongs of the old bell slowing down.'"*[88]

We can return before God again and again, like Corrie, and pour out our emotions and thoughts. "I AM WHO I AM" will make gems out of our turmoil.

"With-ness" will come. The people who will come alongside us are gifts from God, whether old friends or passing strangers. Tenacious trust in Him will not disappoint. He supplies the human "with-ness" we need, not expect. Gratitude, humility, and forgiveness open passage for grief's deeper work in us.

The How of
Anticipatory Grief

Torn over time
Brown curls and dies
Buried in white
The wind alone cries

White disappears
Sun warms Brown's tomb
Rain and wind kiss
Make Brown Green's womb

CHAPTER 9

The Wind of Mercy

*God's mercy is so great that you may sooner
drain the sea of its water, or deprive the
sun of its light, or make space too narrow,
than diminish the great mercy of God.* [89]
– Charles Spurgeon –

Orlando, FL. Jan 4, 2005

Hannah sat on the edge of the couch. Her mouth open. Chest heaving. Eyes wide.

"I. Can't. Breathe."

Fear iced my heart.

She adjusted the oxygen tube in her nose. I jumped up and crossed the room to check the pressure on the canister. Nothing obstructed the air flow.

Please, God, please. I know you can stop cystic fibrosis. Just say the word and Hannah will be healed.

How many times in her twenty-three years did my soul voice those words and receive "No" for an answer?

"Coleman, call 911, and I'll call her transplant coordinator."

I ran into her room, grabbed her phone off the bed and speed-dialed the number.

"Hello? Hello? I am Hannah Pratt's mother. We are calling 911. She can't breathe."

Death gripped Hannah by the throat.

Every fiber of my soul quivered for salvation from the fear I could no longer avoid.

Please, God. Please, show mercy.

People reach out to an all-powerful Being when nothing on earth saves their treasure. When the cry reverberates into heaven then fades to silence, some say, "See? There is no God" or, "If there is a God, He must not care." Temptation to not believe dangles in front of anyone who believes in a personal and loving God at some time in their life. I know. When my father died, my faith hung by one thread of truth. God existed.

We may accept the God of gods authored the Bible. We may find His words full of promise. When death threatens what we love, suspicion niggles the soul. We cry out because we wonder. He says He abhors evil. Why does He not answer? A sovereign being who is love must care enough to intervene and protect His Beloved from evil. That seems the obvious answer.

If it were, God would have denied Satan's heyday on the treasured things of Job. After the devastation of his property and children, Job knelt and said, "The LORD gives, and the LORD takes away." His voice rang with certainty, "Blessed be the name of the LORD." [90]

Wasn't his response enough evidence of his faithfulness to God? Didn't he suffer enough loss? But God permitted Satan to attack Job's body. Unrelenting physical pain consumed his body. His mind percolated while he sat on the ash heap. Something transpired in his heart. At the end of the customary days of silence, he carried a mountain range of grief.

Those seven words of misery escaped, "I wish I had never been born."

For the next thirty chapters of his story, Job builds a case for why his pain and suffering are not justified. For every explanation the trio of friends give for why this happened to him, he lays his goodness before them. His practices toward men and his obedience toward God were impeccable. No one, not even God, had evidence against his litany of credentials, so Job believed. Chapter after chapter he claims his pain and suffering unwarranted. He reviews his faith in God's character and worthiness. Surely a just God would honor his righteousness and protect him?

Like Job, I had my list of credentials that night as I watched the paramedics wheel my gasping daughter out on a gurney. We all do. A self-centered justification lodges in all of us. We expect because of His mercy, God will prevent pain and suffering from devastating our hearts—especially if we know Him as *Abba*, the perfect Daddy.

The soul rumbles, cracks, like it did in Job.

Our fists pummel heaven, and we sob, "Why?"

A roar erupts from the soul, "I do not deserve this!"

The heart clutches its treasure in the shadow of death.

Mine did as I stood helplessly watching Hannah suck air.

"She is mine! You gave her to me!"

Yes, God gift wraps goodness and showers it upon us, but not because we earn it. Nor does he withdraw kindness because we mishandle the gift or become undeserving of our treasure. Pain, called anticipatory grief, courses through our veins when death tampers with our happiness.

Why should we embrace the pain? It is not the enemy, but a companion beckoning us to God the source of all comfort. [91]

Sheldon Vanauken in his autobiographical book, *Severe Mercy*, tells a story of love between him and his wife, Davy. Together they were timeless. They attempted a perpetual spring Their love had been a glimpse of heaven. The last stanza of a poem they worked on together describes what they called their "inloveness", impregnable and paramount:

This splendor is upon us, high and pure
As heaven; and we swear it shall endure
Swear fortitude for pain and faith for tear
To hold our shining barrier down the years. [92]

But the barrier broke. A rare disease sucked Davey away. Sheldon wrote he had lost "a glimpse of joy, joy eternal not limited by time" [93] in a letter to C.S. Lewis, a mentor and very close friend, after her death.

Lewis responded, "You have been treated with a severe mercy." [94]

Severe mercy? Such an odd combination of words. An oxymoron. Synonyms for "severe" include "harsh," "rigid," and "cruel." "Compassion" and "clemency" could easily replace "mercy." Should it not protect us and what we love from evil? Should not compassion intervene in our unrelenting pain? Not if something more is at stake. God says "Yes" to a larger vision and purpose when He says "No" to our pleas. All His promises are "Yes" in Christ. [95] Nowhere else.

The wind of mercy rides on the back of our grief.

In the book *The Misery of Job and the Mercy of God*, John Piper imagines Job conversing with his granddaughter years after his losses. She asks if God was mean to him. Unjust. He responds:

The Lord has made me drink
The cup of his severity
That he might kindly show to me
What I would be when only he
Remains in my calamity.
Unkindly he has kindly shown
That he was not my hope alone. [96]

God's mercy ruthlessly pursues what we naturally defy—the destiny for which He shaped us. He is our solace, our rest. Nothing compares to knowing and relating to Him. There is something more merciful than withholding death from what we love. With unkind kindness, He waits, His eye focused on the human will made God-resistant so long ago. The wind bears down in silence.

A mercy as severe as death, a severity as merciful as love.[97]

A psalm writer describes a scenario of devastation often felt in the journey of anticipatory grief: "... the earth gives way and the mountains fall into the heart of the sea. Though its waters roar and foam and the mountains quake with their surging." [98]

When God's goodness and unconditional love do not change our circumstances, He, whose fathering transcends the most loving human father, suddenly seems unfamiliar. Once an intimate friend, He appears farther away than the stars, if He exists at all. How we perceive Him does not define or change Him. The life of our fading treasure does not gauge His character. From the first page to the last, His written story tells His ruthless and successful pursuit of us—His wayward beloved. Pain, suffering, and death cannot deter the Lover of our souls.

We can believe or disbelieve. Regardless of the amount of faith, we are not in control of how our lives become living testaments of the truth. God's story still unfolds in yours and mine—'including anticipatory grief. We, descendants of Adam and Eve, naturally thirst to see what He sees and know what He knows. The sinful soul still expects to share His omniscience and receive a made-to-order brand of His goodness and love.

When He doesn't say "Yes" to our want, we can—and should—express the turmoil of soul. Because of His mercy, we can batter Heaven with questions:

"Isn't there a better way to tell Your story?"

"Where are you?"

We question, and God hears. His silence is not absence. He waits for the soul to exhaust all its self-righteous defenses. God's "No" to the plea for our treasures appears unloving, even vindictive. He could command the sea to heel. His hands could grip the crumbling mountain of our happiness in place. Instead, He keeps His eye on what matters most. With His permission, pain, suffering, and sorrow seep into the soul to crush every person's brand of self-righteousness, watering a different kind of grief.

"Lord have mercy on me, a sinner." [99]

Fighting the mercy of God intensifies the soul's natural enmity toward Him regardless of how strong a belief we have. In *The Wind That Destroys and Heals*, Stephen E. Broyles describes our natural bent and how pain and suffering bring us face to face with what we cannot otherwise see about ourselves. He writes, "The clay man's most outrageous sin is the preposterous presumption that he is powerful. He struts to and from on the earth, imagining that he is the Supreme Being. But no. To feel the frailty of dust is to be disinfected of presumption." [100]

Not until we embrace the mystery of God's omniscience at the bedside of our dying treasure can we see God's mercy riding on the back of our grief. Not until we exhaust our "Why?" will we hear the wind and be comforted by His omnipotence. Not until we let what we fear blow through us as if we were screen doors will our hearts welcome His omnipresence in our darkness. Then, we can hear Him ask us, as He did with Job.

'Who is this that obscures my plans with words without knowledge?
Brace yourself like a man; I will question you, and you shall answer me." [101]

Where was I when He formed Hannah in secret? I was on my knees praying fervently that our child's life would bring God glory. I hoped. Twenty-three years later, I had questions for God. Where was God's glory? This brokenness was not what I envisioned. There was no brilliance of a sunrise and no majesty of a mountain peak. No breath of a miracle stirred.

That night in 2005, as we followed the ambulance to the nearest hospital and waited for guidance from the transplant coordinator, my will crossed its arms and wrestled with the Supreme Being. Sovereign in my world, He did not intervene. A tantrum undermined my confidence in His promises I often repeated to wall out fear and hopelessness. Had I not pursued my part in one I repeated often? Had I not delighted in the Lord? Why did He not give me the desire of my heart? It was my turn to be silent before Abba, whose silence said "No" to my brand of good for Hannah.

Like a forest of grass hiding a chirping grasshopper, the threat of loss looms in front of us. God stands on eternity's height. What Satan intends for evil and disbelief, God uses to unfold His story and reveal Himself to us and through us. When the wind of mercy blows through the cracks of our decaying idea of the way things should be, we can run and try to hide. Once aware of Him and taste of His character, we sometimes wish we could flee from His ruthless pursuit of us.

David wondered in one of his psalms, "Where can I run away from You?"

After imagining possible places he could go, he concludes, "Nowhere." [102]

No personal heaven - or hell. No light of hope. No night of grief. Darkness and evil do not intimidate God. Our night is bright as day to Him. We cannot hide from His love. That is a very merciful thing.

When we let grief crack our demanding spirit, the current of His mercy carries us in our darkness to the height of an eagle's perspective. We can stand with Job, who had no answer to God's questions. We can follow Job's response. "I will put my hand over my mouth." [103]

Our will can bow to the Creator, as did Jesus' in the Garden of Gethsemane.

We can pray his prayer, "Not my will, Abba, but yours be done."

We can plea as He did, "Please, please. If there could be another way."

His Father did not reprimand His Beloved Son, but did not change the plan. Jesus' death was, is, and will be the ultimate mercy toward us. Our sin—our natural presumption the God of gods caters and answers to us—deserves the eternal separation of which dying, death, and darkness give us a glimpse. They are not the end. Life, Himself, could not stay dead.

When we grieve, our resurrected Redeemer says, "I know."

And that is a most merciful thing.

How can we embrace God's severe mercy?

Much like the way a high school friend taught me to embrace the plummeting New England temperatures one Saturday on a beach. She had come to spend Labor Day weekend with me at my aunt's summer cottage. My parents were helping prepare it for the winter.

We had awakened before dawn to walk to the end of the beach before low tide ended. We planned to cross the tidal sandbar, climb to the top of Salt Island and watch the sunrise. Minutes after leaving the house, I was second guessing our plan. My toes burrowed in granules still chilled by night temperatures. A Styrofoam cup somersaulted past us. Sand hissed as the wind skimmed off the dunes.

Head hooded and tucked, I locked my arms across my chest.

If only I had taken the time to put on wool socks and sneakers.

My friend raced across the beach, her long hair a mop whipping in the wind that tossed her words back to me.

"Let go," She spun down the beach, arms stretched like cross beams. "Relax. Stop fighting,"

Really?

"Your body will get used to it."

"Oh, sure," My teeth chattered. I tightened my arms in hopes of saving any warmth.

"Come on! We don't have all day."

I inhaled. My arms relaxed, splitting my cocoon with the flourish of a hatching butterfly. My eyes were closed against the sting of winter. Tears seeped from their corners. With the posture of an unperturbed masthead in the swell of stormy waves, I held my head high, resisting the plea of every part of my body.

Please, please, go back. Everyone else sips hot chocolate and munches fresh warm donuts in a toasty kitchen.

I exhaled. The chill blew through my body as resistant as a screen door.

Take courage. Let the chill of anticipated loss run through you. Acknowledge loss no matter how small. Give emotions — the soul's nerve endings — a voice. Little losses and stress create pressure on our inner world like hands of a doctor pressing around the neck in a routine exam.

She discovers a lump and asks, "Does that hurt?"

Or pain explodes at the pressure point.

When overlooked, emotions gain strength and will express themselves. They infiltrate thinking, control decisions and behavior. Often, they explode. Their debris spills into mundane circumstances and cascades over whoever stands near.

Hot and molten anger rumbles in the depths. It explodes over a chattering child or the driver ahead who travels too slow for our smoldering disposition. Anxiety creeps into what to choose for lunch. Hopelessness twists the heart, smothering energy. An ache to escape beckons. Addictions can develop from innocent attempts to rest from the daily pressure. Innocuous habits like reading, surfing the internet, and browsing social media efficiently build a wall between us and our reality. Favorite fast foods or sweets that supply a tonic of comfort over time can replace daily healthy choices. A sleeping pill, or two, then three offer oblivion.

There is a time to anesthetize distress but not as a way of life. Like water, grief must have a way out. Left unacknowledged and unengaged, post-traumatic symptoms will last longer when loss is final.

Let grief brings tears.

They may escape like an underground stream leaking from a rock face on the side of a mountain while waiting for the doctor's prognosis in a hospital room. They may gush like a cracked dam while driving home with freshly printed divorce papers in the passenger seat.

Tears need not be signs of weakness or victimization, but of courage and humility. They soften a sullen heart. Their saline drenches a wounded one. They are the voice when words are insufficient. Facing the sealed tomb of Lazarus, fully human and fully God, Jesus wept. [104]

Yes, He knows. Jesus' "in-to-me-see" completely invades our darkness. There is nowhere He has not been. He does not judge our tears. David, in his poetic style, depicts that God does not discount our tears. Instead, He has "...kept track of my every toss and turn through the sleepless nights, Each tear entered in your ledger, each ache written in your book." [105]

Words give grief a powerful voice, as they did for Job, David, and Jesus. Verbal venting does not necessarily sabotage the deep work of mourning, but its force is best contained in a safe place. As I said in the previous chapter, a friend who listens in silence gives priceless "with-ness." This kind of relationship is rare and should be proven in smaller matters of "in-to-me-see." A counselor or a spiritual mentor may also be that friend as long as the goal is not to fix and move on. Their ears and eyes can be the ledger to enter tears and their mind and heart can be the book.

God listens. David, shepherd-turned-king, journaled his grief over and over again in poetry. In our inner upheaval, we can benefit from reading psalms of lament where David and other writers pour out their souls as they stand in the chasm between personal reality and what their faith knows or does not know of God's nature. We, too, can journal our emotions and faith that toss about like

Styrofoam cups on windy days at the beach. We can address our words to Him. God knows our raw state. Being honest opens our depths to unacknowledged truth about ourselves and our relationship to Him.

Like Jesus, we can pray aloud and loudly. On a beach, in the woods, at the top of a hill, or behind closed doors, we can cry out. Though He may be silent, though He does not intervene, His wind of mercy will steer our grief into His lap of grace.

CHAPTER 10

The Seed of Trust

*Our silence is the door for God to enter ... Grief
can roar at such a pitch that God seems silent
But He is not.* [106]
– Calvin Miller –

Easter, 2005

My brother-in-law walked to the pulpit, straightened his notes one final time.

He put on his reading glasses and began his sermon:

Last January my niece, Hannah, who has cystic fibrosis, became very ill and had to be life-flighted to Shands Hospital in Gainesville from Orlando. After a few hours there, the doctor asked to speak to Coleman, my brother and Hannah's father. The doctor told us that Hannah was still in danger of going into respiratory distress, which meant for a CF patient that her lungs would be no longer usable. She had already been intubated. He said the only way to save Hannah was to keep her on the respirator. But, if she remained more than three days the change in Hannah's respiratory system would mean removal from the transplant list, which is her only hope of survival. The doctor needed to know what Hannah wanted to do: remain on the respirator or remain on the transplant list.

When we returned to the room, Hannah knew something was going on and wanted to know. My brother sat down on her bed, and told her if she needed the respirator longer than three days, she would be taken off the transplant list.

"He needs to know now, Hannah."

She leaned over, her head bowed.

Trying to think ...

Trying to breathe ... twenty-three years old, and having to decide that.

Then Coleman leaned closer till their heads almost touched and he said, "Hannah, our faith is for moments like this. If it is no good now, what good is it at all? Can I tell you what I think?
"

She nodded. Their heads touched, forehead to forehead.

"I think you should remain on the respirator for three days ... and we will pray and hope the lungs come. And then, if they don't, then, Hannah, I think ... we should remove the respirator ... because, Hannah, I don't want to hold you here like that ... and keep you from the arms of Jesus."

Hannah was still for a moment.

And then, she nodded again. "Yes"

She looked death straight in the eye. She saw its red eyes and yellow teeth. She and my brother stared it down. And she said "Yes!" to trying to live ... "Yes! to having to die ... And "Yes! Oh yes!"to Jesus ... to that brave strong Savior who meets us in every death. He is with us as we walk through the valley of the shadow of death.

Death was sent running for cover that day to this very day. Hannah has gotten better and stronger as she waits for those lungs. Why? What happened? I think it is because, in that moment, when she went forehead to forehead with her father, death did all it could to Hannah. She died. She let go. She sunk into the abyss and she found what is true: whether we live or die, we are the Lord's. When we finally know that, then what is there to be afraid of? [107]

*****

"Nothing, not even death" should be the answer to my brother-in-law's question, but is it?

Death does not lurk in our thoughts during normal days, months, or years, though it follows us from the moment of conception. One day, its shadow crosses our path threatening to take what we love. We muster our defenses. We naturally fight for life as we know it.

At each skirmish, death reminds us, "I will not be ignored."

The beat of eternity in our soul whispers, "Hope... Hope ... Hope ..."

Yes, we should grip hope. We should choose life and remember life flows from and belongs to God. We were made to enjoy life forever—made to overflow with unending happiness — with Him. We cannot outrun death, the final enemy, though we pour ourselves into trying. At the first threat of loss, every heart squeezes with fear and fights for the life it desires.

Anticipatory grief, our faithful companion, nods, "Ohh, yes. Savor life. Fight death, but do not be mistaken. This world's hope disappoints."

So what hope can we cling to? We can cling to the hope our soul cannot see in its insatiable appetite to define happiness - the hope that ensures eternity with God. Our restoration with the Father through Christ Jesus *is* our only hope that does not disappoint.

God becomes God in our lives anyway He desires to be. He is not our friend to do what we ask, to make us happy, nor to keep us from pain. Verses, such as the one I clung to through Hannah's life, are not contracts God makes with us but promises of transformation. To delight in God means placing personal desires and demands under His sovereignty. Release the grip. Let go of ownership—of control.

No need to be afraid. Let death come to self-centeredness.

We have no idea how tight is our hold on a desire until little losses pry our grip bit by bit. The green womb of hope for our treasure beats strong in the early autumn of loss. The heart clings tenaciously as winter creeps closer and the wind grows bitter, as it should. God gave us His capacity to love. Yet, the vision for our desires rises no higher than our will until we submit to His. There is no space for rights in trust.

We naturally clutch our treasure like a sealed pod in summer fat with seeds. We pray for healing. Beg for solutions. A murmur of prayers swells and ascends as we post requests on social media. And when "Yes!" is the answer, happiness bubbles over. And it should.

"No" is an answer, too. The wait for rescue (or final loss) is the soul's autumn of loss. In this spiritual journey the will experiences anticipatory grief. It often begins with the demand for answers. Often the questions begin with "Why ... ?"

"Why is this happening? To me? Why can't I have what I want?"

"Have I done something wrong? How can I make it right?"

Our soul does not politely ask, but it wails and thrashes like an over-tired toddler fighting sleep, unappeased except by yet another helping of milk.

God whispers, "Trust me with all your heart. Do not lean on your own understanding." [108]

Our soul wrestles more and we ask, "What will happen to me if I let go?"

He answers, "Whether I say yes or no to your desire, I have written my law on your heart. I have removed a heart of stone and have given you a new heart, one of flesh, that wants me above all else." [109]

Surrender begins the first time we trust the life of our desire to God. And the second. And third ... Submission takes time like a seed that falls to the ground and dies. [110] In this spiritual journey, our will experiences its own anticipatory grief.

Eighteen months before that life and death conversation in the MICU. Hannah wrote in her journal:

> *What is it in my life that must die? What must be sacrificed to produce new life for others. Lord, please show me. I do not want my life here so much that I miss the wonderful things You have placed in my box! I want to follow you, Christ. I also want to lead others to follow You! May the prayer of my heart be – as Christ prayed – Bring glory to your name! Thank you for the glory already given, and for the continuing work that You want to do IN and THROUGH me? Again, I ask that anything hindering that work would die! I trust you – that You have bigger plans than what I could imagine. I trust that what deaths that must occur are for Your purposes. I do not pretend to understand, but I must commit to trust.* [111]

Yes, Hannah wanted to live. She had dreams. She entered her personal Garden of Gethsemane the day she wrote those words. So do we the moment we open our arms to the wind of mercy. We abandon our longing to the current of God's love like the pregnant milk pod that bursts open.

Life — bad and good — is where He loves us. How does He love? Unconditionally. He promises all things work out for our good, according to His purposes, which is our transformation into the image of Christ. [112] His desire for us transcends the life or death of our specific longing, as well as the length of the wait. Between hope and final loss, He carries our seed of trust wherever He pleases.

For Hannah, that included the life and death crisis on MICU. After six weeks, she stabilized enough to move into transplant housing where I had been staying across from the hospital. Life in Orlando moved on without us. Though home was two hours away, it might as well have been cross country. We lived in a state of temporal permanence. Each day could be the final day of waiting.

Months stretched past a year.

Another weekend had ticked away. I sat on the double bed in the back bedroom. A blank wall loomed in front of me. Dawn peeked through closed blinds. A mockingbird's solo announced another day. Hannah would not be up for another two or three hours. I had just scribbled a fresh tirade of "How long shall we wait?" on the two pages of my journal. My Bible lay open to Psalm 131.

The wall and I had become companions. Each morning the expanse greeted me. It laughed when sunlight tickled its nakedness. When daylight dulled dark, the tungsten glow of lights from the hospital parking lot slid through the closed blinds etching thin diagonal lines across its emptiness. Shadows textured the old pitted face overseeing the room like a watchman waiting for morning.

This Monday morning, in front of my silent friend, I imagined what I had just read:

My heart is not proud, LORD,
 my eyes are not haughty;
I do not concern myself with great matters

or things too wonderful for me.
But I have calmed and quieted myself,
I am like a weaned child with its mother;
like a weaned child I am content.

My soul like a weaned child? What did that look like? The nothingness in front of me seemed to leaned closer, "Wait without wanting."

Adam and Eve had no knowledge of wanting or waiting before they suspected God kept something from them. Waiting for God to arrive in the cool of the day contained no expectations. They anticipated their time with Him. He satisfied them, nothing more. All they needed, He provided.

God warned them against tasting the one thing they did not need - evil. Suspicious of His wisdom and curious what they lacked, they tasted. Their innocence crumbled. Ever since, every person's soul seeks satisfaction elsewhere. We naturally run from Him, desperate to prove we do not need Him. The ache of "never enough" shadows us.

A newborn's cry speaks of our universal dissatisfaction. We are always in want of something. To use "want" in its original medieval meaning, *need* permeates our daily lives. We make to-do lists to keep it at bay, but a dead car battery *requires* a detour in the day's plan. Or, we *lack* milk for tomorrow morning's cereal. Health issues *demand* we interrupt normalcy for a doctor's appointment. We pine for a dog now gone.

We were made to *desire*, but our *wanter* naturally pursues self-defined satisfaction. Objects of desire fit awkwardly in the God-shaped vacuum of the soul. A never-ending chase for happiness, no matter how big or small, ensues daily for a lifetime. We plan and hope, then are disappointed. Capricious and fickle weather spoils a relaxing day at the beach. A disagreement blights a deep friendship. Pain disturbs sleep. A diagnosis changes the trajectory of retirement.

Satisfaction has a shelf life.

A husband's eye roves. We repaint the color of a bedroom. We want just a little more helping of that delicious ...

The earth re-enacts the story of the insatiable *craving*. Plants *thirst* for water and light. *Hunger* drives lizard and lion to forage, and *urges* ants to stock pile before winter. Gazelles and cheetahs congregate at watering holes that *beg* for rain. The howling wolf *aches* for the mate lying dead at its feet.

Needing. Wanting. That is our life, because nothing created was ever meant to satiate the thirsty soul. Only God satisfies.

When hope disappoints — when the ongoing ache remains unrequited yet another day — when our thirst and hunger for its fulfillment gnaws at the hours, months, or years — the wait appears to be our nemesis, but it is our friend leading us to Abba's lap. The insufficiency of everything on this earth leads us to Him, the true place of contentment.

"God is my shepherd, I shall not want," [113] whispered David as he wrote the twenty-third Psalm. His imagination was filled with images from his shepherding days while a teenager. He led the sheep to graze unperturbed in a patch of lush green. Then, he would disturb them. Despite their bleats and scampering, he corralled them with his staff toward a quiet watering hole. He killed a lion and a bear to protect them. Perhaps he got up at night and trekked to the pen to check on them when wolves howled nearby. The light of stars punctured the darkness.

"For You are with me." [114]

This is a guaranteed promise Christ gave his disciples and any person who believes He died, was buried, and rose again for sin. [115] Before His unjust death, He informed His friends He was returning to His Father. He assured them, saying, "I will not leave you as orphans. I will ask Abba to give you another counselor. The Spirit of Truth will live with you and be in you forever." [116]

All of God is present in the Spirit. He searches our darkness and brings sin to light. He opens our understanding to our true want, God Himself. [117] No death can rob us of God including the anticipated loss of our personal desire. We can receive strength moment by moment, day by day, to relinquish its life to severe mercy. He *is* our living hope present when life is happy or sad.

Nine months before Hannah and Coleman's life-and-death conversation Hannah wrote in her journal:

I have been struggling with the whole issue of placing God before all things. I have felt guilty for continuing to have desires for things on earth: to be married, to finish school, or to have some kind of musical career. However, somehow tonight, I believe God gave me a gift. He set my heart at ease. He knows! I am human, so I will have desires for earthly things. Through scripture, though, He tells us to place Him above all. However, He never tells us to place Him instead of all. The true honoring of Christ comes when we do have our own wants, but to choose to hold them loosely or give them up when He calls us to. So it is not that everything else is not important, but that when standing in front of Jesus, I realize they are not most important. They become my second things - which are not invisible or do not disappear — but when compared to the voice and presence of

113

Christ, they are placed in their proper position. If the desires of my heart are placed second to Christ, then through Him I can have clear access to them. Only because He allows me, can I have them. He stands in front of what I want and only allows me to have what He knows is best.

Though desire for God above all else lies in our DNA, it cannot be accessed except by repentance — the grief of the soul that happens while dying to what we want. No one delights in God above all else. With each desire of the heart, everyone's wanter must die—must pass through its own autumn and winter—even spiritual giants like Job and young women like Hannah. When loss consumed their world, their grief led them to worship God. They accepted the truth that He created all things, gives all things, and in Him all things hold together. [118] But there is more to trust than recognizing His sovereignty.

Job's biographer writes a transitional statement at the beginning of his tale of grief, "In all this Job did not sin or charge God with wrong." [119]

Though he announced he wished he was never born and dumped his messy authenticity through thirty-eight chapters. Even as he acknowledged he might die from his physical afflictions, Job trusts.

"Though God kill me, yet I will hope in Him." [120]

In his pain and his darkness, Job reached out to his Creator, still believing He existed. But God saw in his soul what he could not. When Job wearied of seeking answers, God spoke out of the storm. He challenged the man He called righteous to explain God's ways. Job was reduced to silence. He confessed, "I know you can do all things, and that no purpose of yours can be thwarted ...therefore I despise myself and repent in dust and ashes." [121]

With unconditional love, God woos us to a place of silence —
our rightful place of humility and rest — on His lap. With him we
are content like the weaned child. Though it be for a moment (after
all, we are children), we see clearly.

His wind of mercy drops the seed of trust into layers of loss,
tears, and questions. On the mountain of loss, it lies exposed. The
Water of God ruthlessly softens the shell in the days, months, years
of our wait. Life inside incubates.

CHAPTER 11

Packages of Grace

Unfading beauty flows from truth;
earthly beauty radiates the grace of God
– Tracy K Pratt –

Wednesday, September 20, 2006

From my bird's eye view from the window of the hospital room, I saw cars crawling into the hospital parking lot like ants. Behind me, congratulatory emails and cards papered the walls. But, celebrating seemed passé.

Hannah's health digressed.

Fluid cluttered the airways of the new left lung. An oxygen mask covered her face. She ran a low-grade fever. It felt like old times.

I blinked back tears, turned from the window, and faced her medical team.

"We'll get this under control," said the lead doctor before he left to finish morning rounds. Coleman and I, too, had a certainty, but not in the medical prowess and impeccable care. Circumstances could not be trusted. They twisted our hearts in a tangle of hope and despair. The joy of transplant evaporated.

The door to Jesus widened each day. We had our own rendition of a verse in Psalms "Some trust in [transplant]; some in [medication], but we will trust in the name of our God. Some trust in [ventilators]; some in [technology], but we will trust in the name of Yahweh; Some trust in [doctors] and some in [science], but we will trust in the name of our Father." [122]

I found myself breathing hard, willing air into her obstructed lungs. Praying. Begging.

"Oh God, why? Please. Please, protect these precious lungs. Why all these problems? We have waited so long. Hannah has worked so hard."

The ache lodged too deep for tears and was too heavy to carry alone. I escaped to the outside staircase landing to answer a call from a friend. She and her husband had sat with Coleman and myself during the nine-hour transplant surgery. The wind ruffled a pile of brown leaves in the corner. Sunshine spun gold across their surface. Pedestrians crisscrossed paths beneath me like any other day.

I voiced my grief, "Hannah is going to die." The words seemed melodramatic. Surreal.

A sycamore leaf wrinkled with dehydration fluttered to my feet. Life's scars were frozen in brown. Jagged holes and broken edges told the story of ladybugs and caterpillars traipsing over its green expanse. Its gigantic size indicated a feast on sap, sunshine, with draughts of rain. Every line once breathed. Its green faded to brown.

While living in transplant housing, our wait for a double lung transplant moved into spring, summer, then autumn and winter of 2005. I began to see beauty in bits of brown on my walks in the neighborhood around Shands Hospital. Each time an array of treasures stuffed my pockets by the time I arrived "home" at Apt. 24. A collection grew in my bedroom: a cluster of acorns, a piece of bark shed from a sycamore tree. A perfectly preserved magnolia bloom found a home on a straw wreath with other dried treasures. A trio of hickory shells rested on the windowsill, their nuts were long gone before I found them. Mid-morning sunshine spotlighted their hollow space once full of life's promise.

The beauty I saw in the details of these small inanimate "dead" things sung of God's grace. [123] They reminded me to let go and abandon my desires in the way Jim Elliot, a missionary murdered for his faith, describes: "He is no fool who gives what he cannot keep to gain what he cannot lose."

When life ebbs from our treasure, what cannot be lost does shine bright—the wonder and beauty of the way things will be. There will be a happily ever after. With Him. There will be a heaven and earth where beauty does not fade, hope does not disappoint, goodness never ends. God will live with us. There will no longer be a reason for anticipatory grief. He will wipe every tear away. [124] That time will come in His time.

Until then, God is the center of what things are, whether we believe He exists or not, always making Himself, His story, and His world more visible — even in the lines and fading color of that sycamore leaf lying at my feet that day I voiced my grief to my friend.

How natural to fix our eyes on what is tangible and experiential — on machines that keep track of vital signs. We tune the ears to alarms or the ring of a phone when hoping for good news in a bad situation. Another potential life-saving decision evokes manageable hope ... then, another. But the time comes. The inevitable looms. Hope flutters like a leaf broken from stem.

When the Lover of our souls does not intervene in the dying process, He gives a promise, "Nothing separates you from My love not even death of what you cherish." [125]

Anticipatory grief shows us how to watch for evidence of God's presence in our helplessness. It knows where to find grace on the mountain.

Walking stick in his right hand, a backpack slung over his left shoulder, and a sheathed knife clipped to his leather belt, AG strides up to the heart's door. His chapped knuckles rap against the wood. On the other side, the heart takes a deep breath and grabs the doorknob, but stumbles back. With an open palm, AG pushes the door wide and steps through. A swift kick with his left boot slams the door shut. The heart stumbles back.

"You got long johns on?" asks the bearded old man as he pulls up his new charge from the floor. Gloves, cap, and scarf lie on the table.

"Yes."

"Wool socks?"

"Yep."

"Okay, then." AG points to the pile on the table. "You gonna put those on?"

A gust of reality blasts icy air through the heart's bones as AG opens the door. "Do you think I'll be warm enough?"

"Gotta let those shivers take their course." AG exits the door onto the porch and down the steps. His words linger behind him. He crosses the small clearing to the edge of the wood. Leaves crunch and sticks crack under his boots. He pauses to look back when the front door slams. The heart huddles against a pillar on the front porch.

"You comin'?"

With one more tug on the gloves, jacket sleeves, and ski cap, the heart takes a huge breath.

"I'm coming!"

Their words crescendo through the forest's silence.

The heart catches up to AG. His right-hand grips the head of his walking stick deep in a sea of brown leaves. A little smile crinkles the corners of his eyes, his head thrown back. The heart follows his gaze. The trees rise like the buttresses of a chapel. It's ceiling a deep blue sky with bleached white clouds coasting by. Their branches sway in the winds that whistles through the tree tops. Leaves glow like stained glass as the autumn sun filters to the forest floor. The quiet below settles in the heart.

Without breaking his gaze, AG speaks so low he may have been talking to himself, but the heart hears every word:

May all your expectations be frustrated
May all your plans be thwarted
May all your desires be withered into nothingness
That you may know the poverty and powerlessness of a
child
And sing and dance in the love of God who is the Father,
the Son, and the Spirit. [126]

Is knowing the poverty and powerlessness of a child worth dying to our expectations, plans, and desires for our treasure? Is singing and dancing in His love enough? I say, "yes." To know God and to be known by Him transcends our understanding of Him and the answer to our "why's."

The heart's limit is stretched by layers of tension between lost and new normal as well as between hope and loss. How does it survive? It doesn't. It breaks. The helplessness of a child is the new normal. Our trustworthy friend, anticipatory grief, gives no advice. In fact, he speaks little. When he does, it is to spotlight God's "in-to-me-see" affection. No diversion, no matter how good, can remove our dubious companion's presence. On the lonely road, we are never alone. Anticipatory grief's shadow keeps the heart panting after the love of God.

And God is in the center of where we are. Where can we see Him?

Creation sings of His power and divine nature. [127] It is no accident He created the heavens and the earth before He formed His image with the soil of such an insignificant place in universe. Nor did it just happen that the earth's precise location among the planets makes the difference between life and death. [128] What a wondrous display of His protection from the fire of His holiness and a lifeless existence without Him.

Stand in the serenity of a full moon that whispers, "Remember, the Light of the world rules your darkness." [129] Look at the stars that God knows by name. [130] They are not lost to Him in the heavens. These grand and mystical beauties sing, "Trust our Creator's mystery."

Look for the insignificant details on a walk. Notice the tiny flower rooted in a crack that runs across a sidewalk in the city. Its wee, soulless self nods its head, "Our Creator takes care of us. How much more He cares for you, Image of God." [131]

We can hear God speak "I love you," "I see you" among people who speak the language of our broken heart. Every act of compassion, every service well-done, every word of encouragement is an excellent and perfect gift from heaven. [132] In Hannah's twenty-four years, medical staff, pharmacists, and even employees of Social Security were God's hands and feet ministering to our family. Some played significant, lengthy roles. Others were passing encounters that encouraged our hearts like the warmth of home on a cold, windy day. The amount of stories could fill another book.

One particularly hard day, a therapist came to give Hannah a scheduled breathing treatment. I had never met him before. Our conversation meandered into favorite foods. I mentioned cheese grits.

"Have you ever had shrimp grits?" he asked.

"Um-no. I have never heard of that."

His eyes widen. His eyebrows arched. "Never? Oh, I make some mean ones. Next time we have a potluck in the therapy department, I'll bring you some."

"Really? That would be fun to try." I confess I did not expect him to follow through, but a few days later there was a rap on the door.

"Come in." Hannah and I said simultaneously.

He held a paper plate like a silver platter fit for a princess. A plastic spoon and fork stood tall in a mound of white.

"Here you go. Fresh from the pot."

He transferred his gift into my lap. Flecks of pink shrimp dotted the white.

I looked up. He stood grinning.

Oh dear, he expects me to eat it now.

I grabbed the spoon digging deep into the grits and caught a shrimp.

The miniature mound disappeared into my mouth. He watched my face.

"Wha' dya think?"

"Delicious! Thank you." I mumbled through a mouthful.

We never saw him again nor ever knew his name, but he remains in my hall of fame where Abba's "I am right here," still reverberates.

We must give ourselves and others grace to find healthy support outside everyday normalcy. There is no shame in acknowledging when existing relationships are not enough. There comes a time when they cannot be enough.

When Hannah was diagnosed with CF, Coleman and I recognized she was so much more than the faulty genetic makeup that caused the disease. We chose to give her a life not dictated by the prognosis but by God's purpose for which she was created. Everything about her was designed to tell His story. We managed treatments, checkups, and IV therapy with music lessons, school, and sleepovers.

Occasionally we participated in the local Cystic Fibrosis Foundation (CFF) during her childhood, but close adult and peer relationships in church and school seemed adequate support for her and each family member. By the time she was an adolescent, CF's unpredictable rhythm interrupted school and her social life. The distance between the two worlds widened. The rich community surrounding us could no longer provide emotional support. Ever so slowly, Hannah and I had moved into the CF world. It was not until those eighteen months in Gainesville that I experienced the value of knowing other moms of children with CF and witnessed a peace in Hannah as she mingled in the physical therapy gym with therapists and patients.

This is not an indictment on community. All the love, sympathy, and intuitiveness of friends in normalcy cannot speak the language of anyone's particular ache. All the "I know just what you are going through," casseroles, and cards cannot speak with the fluency of an individual who walks parallel or a little ahead of us. People in anticipatory grief go to war to save the life of their treasure. The battles, the tension, and scars take their toll. Fellow fighters know.

Our closest "in-to-me-see" relationships need room for differences in roles, perspectives, and personalities. How we relate to the loss affects how we grieve. Though circumstances of anticipatory grief are the same, each member's sorrow is a dialect of the same language. Family members or close friends cannot be one another's confidante simply because emotions and imagination are too enmeshed in the same circumstances. Respecting privacy and giving each other freedom to seek support says, "I understand I cannot offer you what you need. I am and always will be here in the way I have always been."

December 2004

Hannah's legs dangled off the edge of the examining table. The routine pre-transplant checkup was almost finished. Her coordinator stood at the counter in the corner of the room filling out the chart. All three of us had been making cheerful small talk. A tiny silence invaded the room.

"Hannah, do you have any questions about what to expect during transplant and afterward?" she asked with eyes still on the computer.

I looked at Hannah. She had pulled up her legs and hugged them. Her chin rested on her knees.

"Yes. Could you ... I was wondering ... "

Her coordinator looked up and laughed, "You are tongue-tied?" She put down her pen. Stepped away from the counter. She grabbed the office chair and sat, rolling it directly in front of Hannah. "Ask me anything."

Hannah guarded her internal world like it was Fort Knox. I leaned forward. Here was her chance to get answers. Would she voice them?

She unwound her body. Her fingers gripped the table edge. Her arms stretched like thin rods. "You mentioned awhile ago I could talk to a young man with cystic fibrosis who had a double lung transplant."

"Yes, he'd be very open to talking with you. Right now, he has an infection in his right lung. When it's under control, we can set up a time. Is that what you want?"

"Yes." Hannah sat back. "Thank you." Her hands relaxed in her lap. Her legs swung gently.

When the coordinator set up the meeting, we agreed to meet the young man in the solarium portion of the lobby. At the appointed time, the four of us sat in a semi-circle barricaded from foot traffic by two wide columns. With introductions finished, Coleman and I excused ourselves and moved our chairs closer to the stream of activity.

A wall of camaraderie shielded the two from the rest of the world. They sat behind us, silhouetted against the flurry of cars beyond the plate glass windows. Their chairs respectfully distanced to avoid germs, Hannah's mouth was moving fast. She leaned forward. Gestured with her hands. She leaned back. He leaned forward. His lips moved. She nodded. They laughed. At one point, Hannah shifted in her seat. A single recessed light cast its beam directly on her face. It glowed with a radiance of peace, of a deep longing finally satisfied.

This brief encounter with a fellow traveler filled a hole in Hannah's soul that no professional and no loved one could. Commonality with our loved ones has limits which we must recognize as a sacred boundary. We each need those who speak our dialect.

In anticipatory grief, we can assume a good relationship, no matter how brief, is a perfect gift from Abba. Most encounters are seasonal. Professionals get new jobs. We part from fellow pilgrims and enter new normal, or return to our former ones. In the moment, they are gifts to enjoy. Each is a package of grace much like autumn's harvest piled high at a roadside stand. Savor them like the sweet smell of a freshly picked apple. Feast on the camaraderie like a trio of pumpkins casting a cheery glow from a front porch.

At the end of every day, in the powerlessness and poverty of a child, we can remember where and from whom we have heard God say, "I see. I know." Review the day. The simplest gifts are worth celebrating. The packages of grace witnessed in word, deed, or object make the music to which, on recollection, the heart can dance in His love and sing, "Thank you."

CHAPTER 12

The Way of the Chrysalis

I shut my eyes in order to see [133]
– Paul Gauguin –

October 2006

The doctor moved Hannah back to Cardiac ICU. She gradually disappeared under life support. Once again, a tracheotomy and ventilator helped her breathe. A feeding tube gave nourishment. Another machine drew infection from the left lung. Medications were added, subtracted, adjusted. She slept more, communicated little, and used sign language when she did. I interpreted.

At one point I shook my head, bewildered, "Hundreds pray for Hannah, and the journey seems to be getting worse."

Coleman agreed, "How much can a human being take? What recourse do we have except to go to Hannah's Creator?"

One afternoon a hint of her perky self peeked through. I sat in a camp chair at the foot of the bed. Her hospital bed was tilted just enough for her to lay slightly propped. A frame of pillows encased her body. She gestured to me.

A spark of life glowed in her eye. She moved her arms in a series of signs.

I leaned forward. "Say that again? Slower."

She pointed to herself.

"I."

With one decisive movement, she swatted her left fist with her open right hand.

"Struck down."

Her eyes widened. Her head nodded ever so slightly. She gestured like a baseball umpire signaling a runner is safe.

"Not."

She paused. Seemed to sit up straighter, then made her last sign with such vigor, the bed jiggled.

"Destroyed." I interpreted. "You are struck down, but not destroyed."

She nodded.

"Yes, Hannah. Yes!"

In those few seconds, Hannah's soul sang above the conflict. The notes rang clear. The Light that shines out of darkness filled Hannah's deteriorating body. In her impoverished state, she sang and danced in the love of God who is Father, Son, and Spirit.

She closed her eyes. Grace lingered in the hospital room. When physical life ebbed, eternal life burned in Hannah's soul.

Hannah quoted from the Apostle Paul, whose heart God changed from hater of Jesus to lover. "But we have this treasure in jars of clay to show that this all-surpassing power is from God and not from us," he wrote in a letter to the church at Corinth. "We are hard pressed on every side, but not crushed; perplexed, but not in despair; persecuted, but not abandoned; struck down, but not destroyed." [134]

A heart in anticipatory grief knows what it means to be hard-pressed. The compounded tension between hope and loss presses in from all sides. The absence of answers or resolution causes the heart to furrow its brow with perplexity. Barraged by pain and suffering and chased by loss, it does feel persecuted. Worry, fear, and self-pity strike relentless blows.

Though it breaks, the heart is not the treasure the Apostle Paul speaks of but the container. He describes the contents in earlier verses in a layered picture. "And God, who said, 'Let light shine out of darkness,' has shone in our hearts to give the light of knowledge of the glory of God in the face of Christ."[135] The God, who said, "Let there be light" [136] on the first day of creation, resides in the one who believes in Him. [137]

In our darkness, we can know without a doubt we will not die when our treasure dies. A look at the sunrise after a wakeful night reminds us His faithfulness remains unbroken. Every day the sun comes up even when clouds obliterate its blazing glory. Every morning His mercy is new. [138]

Instead of growing cold and wizened with bitterness, despair, and other elements of isolation and disbelief, the heart can spotlight the glory of God without us even knowing. When loss frustrates expectations, thwarts plans, and withers desires, grief makes us His living portrait of Jesus. Messy faith that illuminates Him is much like the transformation of a caterpillar.

One Friday during residency in transplant housing, Coleman and I sat silently by the path that meandered through the Butterfly Rainforest in Gainesville. Sun filtered through the two-story, screened-in space. Voices floated to the sky. Butterflies flitted from one perch to another. The stream gurgled. A butterfly landed on Coleman's shoulder. With mechanized precision its wings silently opened and closed revealing the fine lines and patterned detail. Its rhythm remained unfazed by the voice that shattered our reverie.

"Guess you didn't know you'd attract a butterfly today." A man had stopped on his way up the walkway. A museum employee tag swung against his bright blue shirt. Dialogue bounced between us. We asked questions. He answered.

At one point I said, "It's so amazing how such a different creature can come from the caterpillar."

The museum staff member nodded, "Scientists differ on explanations, but agree the caterpillar dissolves into a DNA soup. Whether it is from a restructuring of the DNA or a different DNA that lies dormant until the caterpillar dies, the butterfly emerges a new creature." [139]

His response made our thoughts fly to DNA language the Apostle Paul used in his Corinthian letter: "Therefore, if anyone is in Christ, he is a new creation. The old has passed away; behold, the new has come." [140]

In the chrysalis of anticipatory grief, grace is at work. It leads our protective and promotional self into dissolution like the caterpillar that moves into hibernation. What happens to our hearts we cannot do ourselves. We can repurpose, repair, or nullify feelings, but we cannot produce the God-life that blooms within the pressure of circumstances and emotions. We are being made into a new creature, in the likeness of Christ Jesus.

Therefore we do not lose heart. Though outwardly we are wasting away, yet inwardly we are being renewed day by day. For our light and momentary troubles are achieving for us an eternal glory that far outweighs them all. So we fix our eyes not on what is seen, but on what is unseen, since what is seen is temporary, but what is unseen is eternal. [141]

The circumstances he describes can easily be a personal breaking point when death's reality leaves no room for rescue. We can accept that truth and not be filled with hopelessness if our eyes are fixed on what is unseen.

How do we fix our eyes on what is eternal while fighting for the life of our dying treasure? We sharpen our acuity by developing an eye for Jesus. [142] Our spiritual eyesight need not be 20/20 on the journey. It can't be in darkness or fog. God gives us the light to move forward one day at a time—one moment at a time. Jesus said that faith the microscopic size of a mustard seed is enough. [143]

We exercise faith in the simplest prayer.

"Why?" yelled in His direction acknowledges His existence. So does a whispered "Thank you, God" at a sunset's beauty that bathes a weary spirit.

"Please, will you ...?" repeated with the veracity of a child asking for a treat in the grocery store expresses belief in His power and ability to hear.

Recitation of the Lord's Prayer before a meal brings to mind His provision for the daily needs of body and soul.

"To fix our eyes" requires margin, a standard requirement in publication, and a necessity in our lives. As you read this book, you benefit from margin every time you come to the end of a line, then drop your eye down to the next line. The space that surrounds the block of content gives your eyes a teeny tiny necessary rest. Bloggers are encouraged to separate paragraphs with white space for easier reading. A well designed website will easily lead the viewer's eyes through a page with generous margin.

Richard A. Swenson, MD wrote a book called *Margins* in 1992. He defined "margin" as the gap between rest and exhaustion. [144] He wrote, "Mental torment hurts. Stress hurts. Overload hurts. Crime and violence hurts. Divorce hurts. Poor parenting hurts. Abuse hurts, sexual diseases hurt. Alcoholism hurts. Drug addiction hurts. Abortion hurts. And when you add up all the hurts, we hurt more than we used to." [145]

Twenty-six years later, cyberspace is the new highway of information. Technology bombards us with more answers than questions. Life expectancy has lengthened. All the circumstances Dr. Swenson listed still hurt. More progress has not eliminated our pain. We need that gap between rest and exhaustion more than ever, especially in the season where death tugs against hope.

What valuable space exists quickly disappears for a person marginalized by waiting, emotional high's and low's, and unexpected turns. Anticipatory grief creates a life overloaded with pressure. Physical and emotional margins run in the red.

There are counter-intuitive choices available that provide breathing room in our internal world. The first is the practice of contentment which restores what demand spends. We are highly susceptible to discontentment in the wait—prone to hurried sickness.

In the wait, regardless of how great the yearning for relief or how bad the news, it is possible at the end of yet another day to say, "God, you are enough. You being here is enough." Our feelings may be contrary to the statement. Regardless, it is true. God is there in the littlest things of life that are big to us.

We increase our vision for the omnipresent God when we repeat His promise to ourselves, "I will never leave you nor forsake you." [146] In the car. At the grocery store. Walking down a hospital corridor or entering the divorce lawyer's office. A tenacious grip on

God's omnipotence gives us strength to take a deep breath when unexpected news twists the heart.

Gratitude expands contentment. Every illumination of grace is worth noting. Perhaps there was a "no" today, but a friend's text or card gave encouragement. People serve us daily in public restrooms, at the crosswalk, in the serving line at the cafeteria, or keep the salad bar fresh and full. Expressing thanks weakens independence and pride which inflate our sense of importance and steal emotional margin. A look in the eye , and a "thank you" breathe kindness into their day and ours.

A litany of thanksgiving to God for the day's goodness (no matter how small) fills the imagination with goodness and waters the tap root of trust as we close our eyes.

Listen for hurriedness. We live in the moment—the space that exists right where we stand. If, in that small space of time, anger or impatience rumbles, slow the pace. Inhale and exhale slowly. Small acts of kindness suspend hurriedness. Look the cashier and bagger in the eye and smile. Make space for that pushy driver forcing his car into the stream of rush hour traffic. Step aside for another to exit the elevator.

Take moments to enjoy life with others and alone. Play. Make good memories in the new normal. Laugh. Invite new acquaintances in similar circumstances to a game night, or meet for dinner and light conversation. Sit in quiet. Go to a favorite outdoor spot. Let the sounds and sights filter out the dirge of "have to," "have not," and "what if." Create. No type of work is better than another. One person tinkers with cars. Another builds models. Others write, cook, paint, or quilt. Working with the hands is a God-given blessing for every person.

Simplify life. Make room for anticipatory grief's emotional monopoly and daily occupancy. This requires strength to say "No" or "not now" to positions of long standing. Watch out for codependency, the need to be needed. It is tempting to think that the journey we are on is less than the work we do and the influence we make. The book club may fold. The number of piano students may need be reduced. The writing life may be shelved. It may be time to end weekly meetings. In His sovereignty, God provides for others who have been dependent on us. We are not indispensable.

We should not wait until resentment or anxiety build to a sudden "I quit" or to the point the quality of our job is affected. We need not wait for a replacement, nor stall until circumstances become urgent. Nor should we expect others to understand the gravity of the decision even if we inform them. The new normal uproots the old. Courageously let go of what is no longer priority.

We should not diminish our situation. It is what it is. Anticipatory grief is nonnegotiable. Quitting responsibilities, letting go of relationships that do not assist in the changes, and creating emotional margin are wise boundaries, though they may appear weak or self-centered. What others think and how they may react is God's business not ours. We must let God do His work in them.

Be assured, there will be fewer or no regrets when we release what is behind us and embrace the journey. The decision is an act of rest in God's sovereign grace. Nothing we do can compare to the sacred and solitary call to climb the mountain of loss in autumn.

Jesus tells us *and* shows us the "way of the chrysalis" is the way of submission to the Father's will. In the Garden of Gethsemane, He placed His life and His death under His Father's authority. He then turns to us, the weary and heavy-laden, and promises "Take my yoke upon me, and learn from me. For I am meek and lowly of heart, and you shall find rest to your souls. My yoke is easy and my burden is light." [147]

Paul Miller, in *The Praying Life*, says, "To become more like Jesus is to feel increasingly unable to do life, increasingly wary of your heart...The very thing [we] are trying to escape—[our] inability—opens the door to prayer and grace." [148] In anticipatory grief, we are increasingly helpless to save the life of our treasure. Regardless of how great the heart breaks, we are not alone. The Spirit of God is here. [149] For those who believe in Jesus, the Spirit lives in us. [150]

In his 1828 dictionary, Noah Webster writes that the root of the word "submission" comes from two Latin words. *Sub*, which means under or below. *Missio*, the verb for "to send" means to submit is a volitional act by the person yielding to another's right to a position or a projected outcome. "Take my yoke" and "Learn of me" are not done to us but by us.

Scripture sharpens our spiritual acuity for Jesus' yoke in our personal chrysalis. God's Word changes us more than any wise words written and provides the soul a feast of life-giving bread slathered in truth sweeter than honey.

The Bible restores light to the eye, strength to the heart, and hope in grief. [151] We open the pages, and the Holy Spirit fills our minds—our imaginations—with the thoughts of God. Sit in the gospels, the biography of Jesus' earthly life. Or read a Psalm a day. The ancient words resonate with emotions, declarations of doubt, and the ring of confidence in God. In many Psalms, the writers' voices rise in a wail or in laughter. Some plead the worst on their enemies.

Journaling is an excellent way to develop a habit of reading His Word. Writing the date at the beginning of a journal entry marks the "way of the chrysalis" like a surveyor mapping uncharted territory. The conversation with Him evolves on the journal page as we "thrite" on a particular Scripture. What word or phrase stands out? Is there an emotional reaction? Does it challenge, confuse, comfort?

Be curious without demanding answers. Write down questions that rise out of the day's reading and circumstances. Record observations. Does the passage speak of God's character? His nature? Is there a promise? An instruction or command?

The Spirit does not fault us for what we don't know. Regardless of our spiritual maturity, a steady diet of Scripture supplies the nutrients that strengthen us in the autumn of loss. These timeless words of God supply our soul with basic nutrients like honey [152] and wholegrain bread do to the body. [153]

We need not have theological prowess or biblical knowledge for God to speak—only a child's faith in Papa's words. It is the Spirit who searches all things and the deep things of God. It is He that reveals the thoughts of God to us. [154] We are the students no matter how little or how much biblical knowledge we have. He is the Teacher. [155] Scripture provides nourishment like milk to a baby or steak to a grown man. [156] If parts of the Bible are too meaty, in time He gives wisdom. Leave them. Or, follow references in the margin or the footnotes at the bottom of the page, which often lead to delightful discoveries.

All Scripture profits "the way of the chrysalis". In anticipatory grief we are powerless. Weariness descends. Faith can grow thin. Reality thrusts a knife into the heart. God's word strengthens our vision to see the unseen.

Sometimes we turn up our spiritual nose at the content that may be difficult to digest, like God's answer to Paul, who asked three times to be freed from a "thorn in the flesh." God said, "My grace is sufficient for you." His thought was not complete, "for my power is made perfect in weakness." [157]

Other passages wash over us in our darkness, such as this promise of His tenacious Presence in Psalms. It can be a comfort, or not, if we wish to hide from Him:

Where can I go from your Spirit?
Where can I flee from your presence?
If I go up to the heavens, you are there;
if I make my bed in the depths, you are there.
If I rise on the wings of the dawn,
If I settle on the far side of the sea,
even there your hand will guide me,
your right hand will hold me fast.
If I say, "Surely the darkness will hide me
and the light become night around me,"
even the darkness will not be dark to you;
the night will shine like the day,
for darkness is as light to you." [158]

One day, the transformation of every soul that trusts in the finished work of Christ will be complete. At the death of a believer, the soul's DNA will be like Jesus'. The butterfly will fly. Effortlessly.

Until then, we travel the "way of the chrysalis" in autumn. Winter is coming. A harvest of metaphors of God's unending goodness and Presence surrounds us:

I am Dawn. Meet Me.

I am Dusk. Sit with Me.

I am Day. Walk with Me.

I am Breath. Inhale Me.

I am Sun. Face Me.

I am Shade. Rest in Me.

I am Moon. Notice me.

I am Life. Live Me.

I am Rhythm. Dance with Me.

I am Wind. Ride Me.

I am Fragrance. Wear Me.

I am Wine. Savor Me.

I am Bread. Digest Me.

I am Lightening. Be in awe of Me.

I am Rain. Drink Me.

I am Truth. Believe Me.

I am Rock. Stand on Me.

I am Wild. Follow Me.

I am Rose. Delight in Me.

I am Music. Listen to Me.

I am Light. Walk in Me.

I am Fire. Fear Me.

I am Brown. Die like Me.

I am Blue. Be at Peace with Me.

I am Green. Embrace Me.

I am Purple. Worship Me.

I am Sapphire. Find Me.

I am Gold. Value Me.

I am Wisdom. Buy Me.

I am Laughter. Join Me.

I am Tears. Use Me.
I am Love. Fall into Me. [159]

We brace against gusts of severe mercy while tramping deeper into loss. God's grace surrounds us more breathtaking than a deep blue sky and the shimmering reds and yellows on a golden day in autumn. When our treasure dies, trust in God lies through winter impregnated with His hope that does not disappoint.

New life will happen in God's time. Spring will come.

The Gift of Anticipatory Grief

Green births Yellow
Purple and Red
They dance in the wind
Where Brown lay dead

Epilogue

What is it in my life that must die?
What must be sacrificed to produce new life
in others? I trust that what deaths that must
occur are for Your purposes. I do not pretend to understand, but I
must commit to trust. [160]
– Hannah Pratt –

October 13, 2006

Coleman and I stood by Hannah's bed. Life support, meant to assist her body in accepting the new lungs, now prolonged her death. The nurse told us her heart had stopped earlier that morning. Hannah had asked for us after the doctors revived her. But, now she was comatose.

We held hands and sang "This is the Air I Breathe", "It Is Well With My Soul", bowed our heads, and gave her back to God. We nodded to the nurse. The noise stopped. Hannah's chest stopped rising and falling.

"Fly, Hannah. Fly to Jesus." We wept. "You're free, Hannah. Go to Abba!" We wept some more.

Coleman and I attended Grief Share in January 2007 where we learned the language and nature of grief among a community of grievers. It is there we heard the term "anticipatory grief." The group met once a week. The other days we worked through content in a workbook that helped process personal grief. The following session would include sharing in small groups. Grief Share gave us a safe place to expose our raw grief and equipped us for the extensive winter of loss that lay ahead.

Most northerners move to Florida after they retire. They are finished with winter temperatures and snow. I married a Florida boy. We have lived thirty of our thirty-nine years in his native city. I do miss winter's stillness, its stark beauty, and how on a hike the bite of Arctic air invigorates. Boots plow through leaves or snow. Layers of clothing from head to toe insulate against the cold. Breath escapes in a miniature cloud. A cardinal's solo pierces the cold air. Bulbs sleep. Something stirs the leaves nearby. Then, there is silence. Stripped bare, the trees' skeletons stand like cast iron sculptures silhouetted against the sky. They are not dead, but dormant. A lull blankets the forest. Autumn's leftovers lay bare to the elements.

Grief after death is like that. The new season takes its course. Though the length and severity differ, we each will have our winter, the time to grieve the bitter cold death brings. It's icy breath blew fiercely into the vacuum that now existed in my internal world. Giving Hannah life had been my life. I now plodded with grief in the winter of loss. Wandering. Disconnected.

One ... two ... three journals and more grew fat with words, pictures and typography expressing emotion, and written prayers. I collected bits of nature that spoke "hope" and added them to the pages. Bits of memorabilia and photos of comforting events mingled among them.

My winter moved into spring when new life was born from the death of my treasure. God's answer to Hannah's prayer of 2003 has been a resounding "Yes" in my family. Our son, JP, met our daughter-in-law, Teresa, in the autumn of 2009. They married in 2011. The unused transplant foundation money seeded by our financial advisor provided funds for them to adopt two children.

Hannah was passionate about protecting and celebrating children in the womb. Her song "For Those Who Have No Voice" has been used on numerous times at a fundraiser for a local women's pregnancy clinic.

In October 2017, I and my family saw God say a resounding "Yes!" in such a way that life will spring from death exponentially. Two other deaths occurred to make this possible — my mother in early 2015 and Coleman's father in the spring of 2016. Because of their lives, love, and generosity, we were able to contribute the initial funds toward the purchase of a mobile pregnancy clinic named "Hannah"

This book, my art work, and creative brand, are also an answer to Hannah's prayer. They celebrate the good story of God found in broken, insignificant, and sorrowful places.

*****

Hannah did not know to what extent she would experience dying to self when she wrote that prayer in her journal. Neither did Davey Vanauken, Sheldon's wife. One night before she was diagnosed with the life-shortening virus that caused her death, and prior to any symptoms, she wrestled in prayer. She offered up her life: "... she humbly proposed holy exchange. It was between her and the Incarnate One." [161] Her spring and Hannah's began when they relinquished their lives to God on the eve of their greatest suffering. Sheldon's blossomed when he met the severe mercy of God in his grief after her death.

We have no idea how God will bring life from the death of our treasure. "What" and "how" are not our business. Under the layers of our autumn new life sleeps through our winter. It is the "way of the chrysalis." We are the vessels in which God pours in—and out—His life. We need not understand or be in a hurry, but simply commit to trust.

Resources for Anticipatory Grief

Caregiving

Caregiver.com: website that provides "an online home for caregivers including tips sections, discussion lists, breaking news, topic specific channels, expert answers and email newsletters."

Jimmie Aaron Kepler, *Thy Will Be Done, 60 Prayers for the Chronically Ill* (jimmiekepler.com, Jimmie Aaron Kepler, 2017)

- A person confronting a chronic illness may feel uncertain about the future. Their hopes and dreams may be placed on hold or have to be altered. They may feel hopeless and helpless.
- Thy Will Be Done: 60 Prayers for the Chronically Ill is a resource to help persons connect with the perfect love which casts out all fear, the love of Jesus Christ.

excerpt from back book cover

Troubled Children

Dena Yohe, *You Are Not Alone: Hope for Hurting Parents of Troubled Kids* (Colorado Springs, Colorado, Waterbrook Press a division of Random House, 2016)

- You would go to the ends of the earth for your child. So, if your teenager or young adult is in the midst of crisis due to self-injury, mental illness, depression, bullying, or destructive choices, you probably feel broken, powerless, and isolated.
- Dena Yohe wants you to know you are not alone. You are not a bad parent. And you are going to be okay... It is possible to find

purpose in your pain, joy beyond your fear, and hope for every tomorrow.

excerpt from Amazon page

Available on Amazon

Divorce

Linda Rooke, *Broken Heart On Hold: Surviving Separation* (Colorado Springs, Colorado, David C. Cook, 2011)

In the '90s after more than twenty years of marriage, Linda W. Rooks and her husband Marv suffered through a painful three-year separation. But, unlike many couples, their story had a happy ending. They reunited in 1998 with a stronger marriage than before.

Because they have experienced the pain of a severe marital trauma but also found the hope of restoration, they are eager to share that hope with others. Having the correct formula is not enough. A person in marital crisis needs emotional and spiritual strength to get to the other side. In Broken Heart on Hold, Surviving Separation, Linda shares from her heart and her experience to help those in marital trauma find relief. She is there to walk beside the reader to shed light in the dark tunnel of marital breakdown.

excerpt from Amazon page

Available on Amazon

Soul Care

Tracy Pratt, Artful Soul Care, blog at www.tracykpratt.com, offers education, inspiration and journal prompts for everyday living with anticipatory grief.

Dr. Larry Crabb, *Shattered Dreams* (Colorado Springs, Colorado, Waterbrook Press, 2001), first edition. This is a book that will...

- draw you to your closest Friend,
- help you discover your deepest spiritual desires,
- point you to your greatest hope,
- help you face your deepest pain,
- and invite you to your highest joy.
- Join Larry Crabb on a life-changing adventure of encountering God in the midst of life's most difficult times. And learn to live beyond your Shattered Dreams.

excerpt from Amazon page
Available on Amazon

Edie Melson, *Soul Care When You Are Weary* (Friendswood, Texas, Bold Vision Books, 2018

Our lives are busier each day, and the margin we have available for recovery and peace is shrinking. Edie Melson helps you find Soul Care solutions using devotions and prayers and opportunities for creative expression. She has learned that sensory involvement deepens our relationship with the Father and gives rest to our weary souls.

excerpt from Amazon page
Available on Amazon

Bibliography

[1] Author's journal entry, October 2003

[2] Coleman and Tracy Pratt, 2007

[3] Genesis 2:15-25, biblical source for author's creative nonfiction

[4] C. S. Lewis, *Mere Christianity* (New York: Macmillan Company, 1970)

[5] Genesis 3:10-1

[6] Genesis 3:3-2

[7] Genesis 3:4

[8] Genesis 3:10-14

[9] Ecclesiastes 3:1-2a

[10] Ecclesiastes 3:4

[11] Psalm 139:13-16

[12] C.S.Lewis, *A Grief Observed* (New York, Seabury Press, 1961), 52

[13] Genesis 3:22, The Message

[14] John 3:16

[15] Genesis 4:15

[16] Genesis 4:9-10, author's paraphrase

[17] Genesis 4:15

[18] Genesis 6:19-20;7:2

[19] Genesis 8:21-22

[20] Genesis 22:7-8, author's paraphrase

[21] Genesis 22:9-13, author's paraphrase

[22] Exodus 1:8-15

[23] Exodus 12:13

[24] John 11:25-26

[25] Matthew 26:38

[26] Ephesians 1:4-7

[27] John1:29

[28] Luke 22:44

[29] Luke 22:43

[30] Matthew 27:46

[31] II Corinthians 5:21

[32] Author's journal, October 2003

[33] C.S. Lewis, *The Great Divorce* (New York, New York, Macmillan Company, 1946), 36

[34] Darlene Gratham, hospice nurse, used with permission

[35] Julian of Norwich, Showings (ca. 1342–ca. 1416)

[36] Revelation 21:3-4

[37] Psalm 46:1-3

[38] Isaiah 53:3

[39] Coleman and Tracy Pratt, 2007

[40] Oscar Wilde, *De Profundis*, 1897

[41] Leigh Wells, illustrator

[42] Time Magazine, January 2007, p. 82

[43] Ibid.

[44] Dag Hammarskjöld, "The World's Best Thoughts on Life & Living," compiled by Eugene Raudsepp,1981

[45] *St. Patrick's Prayer* excerpt, reprinted from www.ancienttexts.org/library/celtic/ctexts/p03.html

[46] James 1:17

[47] Ibid.

[48] Job 28:1-11

[49] Dag Hammarskjöld, *Markings*, 1964

[50] I Corinthians 3:2-3

[51] John Piper, *Think: The Life of the Mind and the Love of God* (Wheaton, IL: Crossway, 2010), 160-161.

[52] Wes Judd, "Conversation With the Psychologist Behind 'Inside Out'", Pacific Standard Magazine (https://psmag.com/search?query=A conversation with a psychologist behind inside out

[53] Job 1:1-19; 2:7-8

[54] Job 2:10

[55] Job 29:2-4

[56] Job 30

[57] Psalm 139:12

[58] Dr. Larry Crabb, in a phone conversation with author's husband, Coleman, used with permission

[59] Exodus 3:14

[60] Revelation 21:4

[61] Genesis 1:1

[62] John 14:6

[63] Proverbs 18:10

[64] Psalm 59:16

[65] Isaiah 64:3

[66] Isaiah 45:9; 64:8

[67] Psalm 71:16

[68] John 14:6

[69] Psalm 103:3; 147:3

[70] Mark 2:1-12; 7:32-35; 5:22-23,35-43

[71] Credited to Oswald Chambers, no direct source found

[72] Jerry Sittser, *A Grace Disguised* (Grand Rapids, MI, Zondervan, 1995), 50

[73] John 9:1-3

[74] Darrell Johnson, *Experiencing the Trinity* (Vancouver, Canada: Regent College Publishing, 2002), 60

[75] Revelation 21:4

[76] C.S. Lewis, *The Problem of Pain* (New York, NY: Macmillan Company, 1970), 93

[77] Matthew 1:1

[78] Mark 1:1

[79] John 1:1-2, 14

[80] Hebrews 12: 4-16

[81] Dr. Larry Crabb, *Soul Talk* (Brentwood, TN: Integrity Publishers, 2003), 46

[82] Wanda Rogers, friend of author, Facebook post, used with permission

[83] Job 2:13

[84] Job 5:17-27

[85] Job 8:1-10

[86] Job 8:1-10

[87] Corrie Ten Boom, excerpt from "Still Learning Forgiveness", Guidepost Magazine ©1972

[88] Corrie Ten Boom, *Tramp for the Lord* (Grand Rapids, Michigan,

Fleming A. Revell Company, 1974)

[89] christianquotes.info; gracequotes.org; relevant magazine

[90] Job 1:21

[91] II Corinthians 1:3

[92] Sheldon Vanauken, *Severe Mercy* (San Francisco, CA, Harper & Row, 1977), 54.

[93] Ibid, 208.

[94] Ibid, 209.

[95] II Corinthians 1:20

[96] John Piper, *The Misery of Job and the Mercy of God*, (Wheaton, Illinois, Crossway Books, 2002), 71.

[97] Sheldon Vanauken, *Severe Mercy* (San Francisco, CA, Harper & Row, 1977), 211.

[98] Psalm 46:2

[99] Luke 18:13

[100] Stephen E. Broyles, *The Wind That Destroys and Heals*, (Colorado Springs, Colorado, A Shaw Books, Waterbrook Press, 2003), 25

[101] Job 38:2-3

[102] Psalm 139:1-12

[103] Job 40:4

[104] John 11:35

[105] Psalm 56:8

[106] Calvin Miller, *The Table of Inwardness* (Downers Grove, Illinois, Inter-Varsity Press, 1984), 72,73.

[107] Sermon, Gwin Pratt, used by permission

[108] Proverbs 3:5

[109] Ezekiel 36:26; Hebrews 8:10, author's paraphrase

[110] John 12:23-28

[111] Hannah's journal entry May 22, 2000

[112] Romans 8:28-29

[113] Psalm 23:1

[114] Psalm 23:4

[115] 4 I Corinthians 15:3-4

[116] John 14:16-18

[117] I Corinthians 2:10

[118] Colossians 1:16-17

[119] Job 1:21

[120] Job 13:15

[121] Job 42:2,6

[122] Psalm 20:7

[123] Matthew 6:28-31

[124] Revelation 21:3

[125] Romans 8:38, author's application

[126] Michael W Smith, Brennan Manning, Carolyn Arends, Rich Mullins, Gary Chapman, Ashley Cleveland, compiled by Jimmy Abegg, *Ragamuffin Prayers*, (Eugene, Oregon, Harvest House Publishers, 2000), 43.

[127] Romans 1:20

[128] Lawrence Richards, *It Couldn't Just Happen* (Fort Worth, Texas, Word Publishing, 1987, 1989), 24; https://www.quora.com/Why-is-the-distance-from-Earth-to-the-Sun-important-for-life-on-Earth

[129] Genesis 1:16, author's application

[130] Psalm 147:6

[131] Matthew 6:28-29, author's application

[132] James 1:17

[133] www.goodreads.com/quotes/180572-i-shut-my-eyes-in-order-to-see; *"Paul Gauguin Quotes."*; BrainyQuote.com, BrainyMedia Inc, 2019 (https://www.brainyquote.com/quotes/paul_gauguin_132609) accessed March 2, 2019.

[134] II Corinthians 4:11

[135] II Corinthians 4:5

[136] Genesis 1:3

[137] John 3:19

[138] Lamentations 3:22-23

[139] https://www.npr.org/sections/krulwich/2012/08/01/157718428/are-butterflies-two-different-animals-in-one-the-death-and-resurrection-theory; https://www.scientificamerican.com/article/caterpillar-butterfly-

metamorphosis-explainer/

[140] II Corinthians 5:17

[141] II Corinthians 4:16-17

[142] Paul Miller, *The Praying Life*, Chapter 11, *Developing an Eye for Jesus* (Colorado Springs: NavPress, 2009)

[143] Matthew 17:20

[144] Richard Swenson, *Margin*, (Colorado Springs, NavPress, 1992).

[145] Ibid., 30

[146] Deuteronomy 31:6,8

[147] Matthew 11: 28-30

[148] Paul Miller, *The Praying Life* (Colorado Springs: NavPress, 2009), 46-47

[149] John 14:15-18

[150] I Corinthians 3:16; 6:19

[151] Psalm 19:7-11

[152] Psalm 19:10

[153] Matthew 4:4

[154] I Corinthians 2:10

[155] John 14:26

[156] Hebrews 5:12-14

[157] I Corinthians 12:8b

[158] Psalm 139:7-12

[159] Author's journal 2003

[160] Hannah's journal entry May 22, 2000

[161] Sheldon Vanauken, *Severe Mercy* (San Francisco, CA, Harper & Row, 1977), 146.

Made in the USA
Monee, IL
25 October 2020

46017729R00100